Praise for Jeffrey Mayer

"Jeffrey Mayer's time management principles save me five to seven hours per week."

> — Jeffrey W. Durkee,
> Resident Vice President,
> Merrill Lynch, Century City, California

"Being able to keep my desk organized and uncluttered all the time is an intriguing prospect. I appreciate your perceptive note and look forward to reading your book, *If You Haven't Got the Time to Do It Right, When Will You Find the Time to Do It Over?* I take some comfort in knowing that many others have been confronted with this problem — and have solved it."

> — Bill Bradley,
> United States Senator,
> Washington, D.C.

"Jeffrey Mayer's *If You Haven't Got the Time to Do It Right, When Will You Find the Time to Do It Over?* is now part of my team's required reading list."

> — Chris Hutchinson,
> Product Development Manager,
> Fisher & Paykel Healthcare, Auckland, New Zealand

"I thoroughly enjoyed Jeffrey Mayer's *If You Haven't Got the Time to Do It Right, When Will You Find the Time to Do It Over?*

> — N.H. Atthreya Ph.D.,
> Director,
> M M M School of Management, Bombay, India

"I thoroughly enjoyed Jeffrey Mayer's *If You Haven't Got the Time to Do It Right, When Will You Find the Time to Do It Over?*

> — Khalid Al-Turki,
> Al Turki Trading, Contracting
> Kingdom of Saudi Arabia

"I loved Jeffrey Mayer's *If You Haven't Got the Time to Do It Right, When Will You Find the Time to Do It Over?*

> — Sarah Hutter,
> Associate Editor, *Working Mother*
> New York, New York

TIME
MANAGEMENT
SURVIVAL GUIDE
FOR
DUMMIES™

by Jeffrey J. Mayer

IDG
BOOKS

IDG Books Worldwide, Inc.
An International Data Group Company

Foster City, CA ♦ Chicago, IL ♦ Indianapolis, IN ♦ Braintree, MA ♦ Dallas, TX

Time Management Survival Guide For Dummies™

Published by
IDG Books Worldwide, Inc.
An International Data Group Company
919 E. Hillsdale Blvd., Suite 400
Foster City, CA 94404

Library of Congress Catalog Card No.: 95-76151

ISBN: 1-56884-972-9

Printed in the United States of America

10 9 8 7 6 5 4 3 2 1

1A/QX/QU/ZV

Distributed in the United States by IDG Books Worldwide, Inc.

Distributed by Macmillan Canada for Canada; by Computer and Technical Books for the Caribbean Basin; by Contemporanea de Ediciones for Venezuela; by Distribuidora Cuspide for Argentina; by CITEC for Brazil; by Ediciones ZETA S.C.R. Ltda. for Peru; by Editorial Limusa SA for Mexico; by Transworld Publishers Limited in the United Kingdom and Europe; by Al-Maiman Publishers & Distributors for Saudi Arabia; by Simron Pty. Ltd. for South Africa; by IDG Communications (HK) Ltd. for Hong Kong; by Toppan Company Ltd. for Japan; by Addison Wesley Publishing Company for Korea; by Longman Singapore Publishers Ltd. for Singapore, Malaysia, Thailand, and Indonesia; by Unalis Corporation for Taiwan; by WS Computer Publishing Company, Inc. for the Philippines; by WoodsLane Pty. Ltd. for Australia; by WoodsLane Enterprises Ltd. for New Zealand.

For general information on IDG Books in the U.S., including information on discounts and premiums, contact IDG Books at 800-434-3422 or 415-655-3000.

For information on where to purchase IDG Books outside the U.S., contact IDG Books International at 415-655-3021 or fax 415-655-3295.

For information on translations, contact Marc Jeffrey Mikulich, Director, Foreign & Subsidiary Rights, at IDG Books Worldwide, 415-655-3018 or fax 415-655-3295.

For sales inquiries and special prices for bulk quantities, write to the address above or call IDG Books Worldwide at 415-655-3000.

For information on using IDG Books in the classroom, or ordering examination copies, contact Jim Kelly at 800-434-2086.

For authorization to photocopy items for corporate, personal, or educational use, please contact Copyright Clearance Center, 222 Rosewood Drive, Danvers, MA 01923, or fax 508-750-4470.

 is a trademark under exclusive license to IDG Books Worldwide, Inc., from International Data Group, Inc.

About the Author

Photo Credit: Roger Lewin

Jeffrey Mayer is one of the country's foremost authorities on time management. For a living, he helps busy people get organized, save time, and become more productive. Jeff's claim to fame is his *clean desk* approach to time management. *USA Today* dubbed him "Mr. Neat, the Clutterbuster," and *People* called him "The Dean of the Desk Cleaners."

He walks into an office, one that looks like a toxic waste dump — with piles of paper, and everything else you can imagine, strewn all over the place — and in two hours the desktop looks like the flight deck of an aircraft carrier. So much has been thrown away that the wastebasket is filled to the brim, overflowing, and spilling onto the floor. All that remains are a handful of file folders, a pad of paper, and a telephone. Everything else is neatly filed away.

Long ago, Jeff realized that if everybody were better organized, they could take more control over their day and would have more time to focus on their most important work. Once they were done, then they could leave the office, go home, and spend more time with their family and friends.

Today, Jeff is paid more than $1,000 for each desk he overhauls. But he's not paid all this money because his clients want to have a nice, neat, orderly desk. The desk is secondary — he's paid all of this money because his clients realize that time is money. And Jeff's able to help them convert time that's wasted during the course of a normal business day into time that can be used more efficiently, effectively, and profitably. Jeff's specialty is in teaching people how to improve their follow-up systems. With a good follow-up system, a person's able to spend more time working on the things that are important, instead of the things that keep him or her busy.

Since the founding of his Chicago, Illinois based consulting firm, Mayer Enterprises, he has helped more than 1,500 men and women get organized and learn how to use their time more effectively. Many of his clients are top executives at Fortune 500 Companies. His corporate clients include Ameritech, Commonwealth Edison, Harris Bank and Trust Company, LaSalle National Bank, R.R. Donnelley & Sons Company, and Sears, Roebuck & Co., just to name a few.

Jeff has been interviewed by almost every major newspaper and magazine in the United States, including the *Wall Street Journal*, the *New York Times,* the *Chicago Tribune,* the *Los Angeles Times, USA Today, People, Newsweek, Forbes, Business Week,* and *Fortune.* And he has been interviewed on hundreds of radio and television programs across the United States, including the *Today Show, American Journal,* CNN, CNBC and ABC News. Jeff lives with his family in Chicago, Illinois.

Speeches and seminars

Jeff would be delighted to speak at your next business meeting, conference, or convention. For date availability, he can be reached at Mayer Enterprises, 50 East Bellevue Place, Suite 305, Chicago, IL 60611. His e-mail address on CompuServe is 74552,157.

Thoughts and comments

If you would like to offer your thoughts or comments about this book, please send them to the above address.

Other Books by Jeffrey J. Mayer

Welcome to the world of IDG Books Worldwide.

IDG Books Worldwide, Inc., is a subsidiary of International Data Group, the world's largest publisher of computer-related information and the leading global provider of information services on information technology. IDG was founded more than 25 years ago and now employs more than 7,200 people worldwide. IDG publishes more than 233 computer publications in 65 countries (see listing below). More than sixty million people read one or more IDG publications each month.

Launched in 1990, IDG Books Worldwide is today the #1 publisher of best-selling computer books in the United States. We are proud to have received 3 awards from the Computer Press Association in recognition of editorial excellence, and our best-selling ...*For Dummies*™ series has more than 12 million copies in print with translations in 25 languages. IDG Books, through a recent joint venture with IDG's Hi-Tech Beijing, became the first U.S. publisher to publish a computer book in the People's Republic of China. In record time, IDG Books has become the first choice for millions of readers around the world who want to learn how to better manage their businesses.

Our mission is simple: Every IDG book is designed to bring extra value and skill-building instructions to the reader. Our books are written by experts who understand and care about our readers. The knowledge base of our editorial staff comes from years of experience in publishing, education, and journalism — experience which we use to produce books for the '90s. In short, we care about books, so we attract the best people. We devote special attention to details such as audience, interior design, use of icons, and illustrations. And because we use an efficient process of authoring, editing, and desktop publishing our books electronically, we can spend more time ensuring superior content and spend less time on the technicalities of making books.

You can count on our commitment to deliver high-quality books at competitive prices on topics consumers want to read about. At IDG, we value quality, and we have been delivering quality for more than 25 years. You'll find no better book on a subject than an IDG book.

John J. Kilcullen

John Kilcullen
President and CEO
IDG Books Worldwide, Inc.

Acknowledgments

A big "Thank you" goes to my publisher, editor, and good friend, Kathy Welton, for all she's done in helping me put *Time Management Survival Guide For Dummies* together.

I would also like to thank my project editor, Tim Gallan, for all of his editorial help, support, and encouragement in writing *Time Management Survival Guide For Dummies*. Tim, it would have been impossible to do this without you.

Another "Thank you" goes to Greg Robertson, my other editor, who offered many great editorial tips that helped to turn this manuscript into a lively, easy to read book; and to Corbin Collins, another IDG Books project editor, for teaching me about the Internet.

And a special "Thank you" goes out to Stacy Collins, Brand Manager, Kathy Day, Publicity and Events Manager, and Polly Papsadore, Director of Marketing, who did just a marvelous job of marketing and promoting this book

And I can't forget the Production people who put this book together, so thanks to Cindy Phipps, Drew Moore, Maridee Ennis, and Gina Scott for making the pages look so good.

I would also like to thank George Bell and Peter Jeff of Steelcase for their help, support, assistance, and insights into the needs of the person who works from home.

And finally, I would like to say "Thank you" to my good friend and computer guru extraordinaire Rich Barkoff, the owner of Ernie's Office Machines in Chicago, for the many hours he's spent over the past several years helping me solve my computer problems and teaching me how to make my computer work.

(The publisher would like to give special thanks to Patrick J. McGovern and Bill Murphy, without whom this book would not have been possible.)

Dedication

To the important women in my life: my mother, Estelle Mayer Loeb; my grandmother, Ida Cohn; two very close friends, Eleanor Brennecke and Magnolia Monroe; two close friends who have recently passed away, Clara Siegel Ehrlich and Pauline Novak; and to my closest friends of all, my wife Mitzi. and my daughter DeLaine

I love you all.

Credits

VP & Publisher
Kathleen A. Welton

Brand Manager
Stacy S. Collins

Production Director
Beth Jenkins

Supervisor of Project Coordination
Cindy L. Phipps

Pre-Press Coordinator
Steve Peake

Associate Pre-Press Coordinator
Tony Augsburger

Editorial Assistants
Kevin Spencer
Tamara S. Castleman
Stacey Holden Prince

Associate Project Editor
A. Timothy Gallan

Copy Editors
Greg Robertson
Michael Simsic

Production Staff
Paul Belcastro
Dominique DeFelice
Maridee Ennis
Drew R. Moore
Carla C. Radzikinas
Dwight Ramsey
Patricia R. Reynolds
Gina Scott

Proofreader
Jenny Kaufeld

Indexer
Joan Dickey

Cover Design
Kavish + Kavish

Contents at a Glance

Table of Contents

Part V: Working in Your Home Office 77

Introduction

Greetings from "Mr. Neat, the Clutterbuster." (Yes, people do *really* call me Mr. Neat.) If you're looking for ways in which to get more work done in less time and with less effort, then you've come to the right place. This book will get you organized, show you how to improve your follow-up systems, and save you time. My goal is to help you get all of your important work done. And when you're finished, you can go home and spend more time with your family and friends.

How to Use This Book

The best way to use this book is to become familiar with it. The first thing you should do is skim it from front to back so you can get an overview of all the timesaving tips, techniques, ideas, and strategies that have filled these pages — in addition to Elwood Smith's wonderful drawings.

Then you should go back to the front of the book and look through the first part on how to get organized. (You may find that you want to actually read this part after you've skimmed it.) And once you read it, you should get yourself a dumpster, throw out all the *stuff* that's been in piles on your desk, and get organized!

After you've done that, I would suggest you keep reading. Every time you pick this book up, you'll discover another tidbit of information that will save you time and help you to become more efficient, effective, and productive. If you feel like writing notes to yourself in the margin or highlighting important pieces of information, I'm encouraging you to do so.

And most importantly, keep this book at your fingertips whenever you need it. Keep it in your desk drawer in your office and carry it with you in your briefcase when you're traveling.

What Are All These Parts?

Part I: Cleaning Up. In Part I, you'll learn how to get organized at the office.

Part II: Working with Your Master List. Here, you'll learn how to master your day with your Master List.

Part III: Using Your Daily Planner. In Part III, you'll learn how to use your daily planner to take control of your day.

Part IV: Working with ACT!. In Part IV, you'll learn how you can take your appointment book, calendar, things to-do list, Rolodex file, and name and address book off your desk and put them all inside your computer with the help of ACT!, the world's leading contact management program.

Part V: Working in Your Home Office. In Part V, you'll learn how to set up your office at home.

Part VI: Planning Your Out-of-Town Travel. In Part VI, I'll give you plenty of out-of-town travel tips.

Part VII: Traveling Abroad. In Part VII, I'll give you some tips for your travels abroad.

Appendix: Frequently Called Numbers. This appendix provides you with a place to write down your most important phone numbers.

Icons Used in this Book

The Tip icon flags a juicy, bite-size bit of information guaranteed to make your life easier.

The Time Saver icon points out the kind of tip that's going to save you gobs of time and add years to your life.

I stuck the Remember icon next to stuff you ought not forget lest a terrible curse befall thee.

The Technical Stuff icon serves two purposes: For people who like fancy-shmancy computer jargon, this icon lets you know where to look. For people who get nervous seeing a digital clock, this icon lets you know that there's stuff you don't want to read nearby.

The Anecdote icon lets you know that I'm about to tell some sort of story, usually a story with a point, but not always.

Part 1

Cleaning Up

Introduction:
Why Should I Get Organized?

We've all heard the phrase, "Time is money," but have you ever thought about how much time is wasted when you can't find that letter, memo, or report that's *lost* somewhere on the top of your desk?

You remember, you were looking at it just the other day. But where in the world did it go? It's got to be here somewhere!? It's got to be in *this* pile. Or is it in *that* pile? Maybe it's in my briefcase.

And, before you know it, 30 minutes have come and gone as you've searched for this lost letter, and you still haven't found it.

Perhaps you've tried to call someone, but you couldn't find the scrap of paper on your desk that had the phone number on it, and you couldn't find the phone number in your Rolodex file because you didn't remember whether it was filed under the person's name or the company's name. And besides, you never got around to putting your Rolodex cards in alphabetical order, so it's almost impossible to find anything in there anyhow. And then again, it may not be in there after all, because you've been too busy to fill out a card.

You probably don't realize it, but most people waste almost an hour per day looking for papers, documents, and files that are lost on the top of their desks — 60 percent of which aren't needed anyway. Wasted time is wasted money. And in addition to wasting this valuable time, they can't remember what work needs to be done and when it's due. With this in mind, I think the logical place to start is with the top of the desk. Because if you want to save time and be more efficient, effective, and productive, you've got to get organized. It's not possible to save time when you can't find anything.

Cleaning Off Your Desk

The fun is just beginning. After you get started, you'll find that it's actually fun to throw things away. And the first step is to separate the wheat from the chaff, or is it the pigs from the cows? Whatever, you're going to go through all the papers on your desk, one piece at a time, and separate the important things from the unimportant ones. If a paper's important, put it in a keeper pile for the time being. (A *keeper pile* is just a new pile you create to hold the papers you want to keep. You don't have to go out and buy anything.) If you've got something that belongs to someone else, create a pile of things to give to your colleagues or coworkers. If you don't need a piece of paper any longer, guess what you get to do with it? Yes, that's right, you get to throw it away! (Of course, this *is* the 90s, and we're all supposed to be environmentally correct, so recycle the stuff that's recyclable.) You'll find that in no time at all — a half-hour at most — you'll be able to throw away at least half the *stuff* that's been gathering dust on your desktop, and it's time to empty the trash.

Do something with the stuff you want to keep

Now it's time to go through your keeper pile to figure out what you want to do with the pieces of paper. Go through the pile, one piece of paper at a time. If there's work to do, you should note it on your Master List, which is a things-to-do list that's written on a big piece of paper. (I know I'm introducing something new here: the Master List. But I'm not going to explain what it is just yet. If you're dying to know about it right now, turn to Part II. Otherwise, just keep reading so that you can learn how to get organized.) If you no longer need that particular piece of paper, throw it away. If you do need it, put it in a properly labeled file folder and file it away. If a folder doesn't exist, create one.

File the important stuff

Here's a novel idea: If you have papers or files you want to keep but don't really need right now, file them away. There's no reason to leave them on the top of your desk any longer. But if you have work to do, don't put anything away before you've noted it on your Master List. (Keep this in the back of your mind because I haven't formally introduced the Master List yet.)

Keep going

Isn't this fun? Did you ever think you could get such enjoy-
ment and satisfaction from throwing away unneeded letters,
memos, reports, and who knows what else? So, now that
you've gone through everything on your desk, it's okay to
keep going. Don't forget about the piles of papers and other
things that have accumulated in your in- and out-boxes — the
ones that have become *hold* boxes on your credenza, your
chairs, the floor, and the window ledge. As you go through all
of these things, you may find that you've got some work to do.
If so, you should put them in your keeper file. If you need to
keep something, put it in a file and file it away; if you don't
need it any longer, throw it away!

Stay focused

Don't forget what your *mission* is: to get organized. So, as you
continue this archaeological excavation of your office, don't
reminisce or interrupt yourself. Your objective is to sift, sort,
and catalog all the things that have been lying on your desk.
You don't want to become distracted or allow yourself to get
sidetracked from the task at hand. When you come across a
note to call someone that has been buried for two weeks —
the note, not the person — don't drop everything to make that
call. Just note it on your Master List and keep going. Or, when
you find a memo that outlined a project you were supposed to
be working on, but haven't yet begun, don't start now. And
when you discover a copy of a letter that you recently sent to
a client, customer, or prospect — and it's been sitting on your
desk for a month — just make a note on your Master List as a
reminder that you've got to make a phone call, and keep
working. These documents are the items of business that
you're looking for. You're going through your piles, one piece
of paper at a time, so that you can create a list of everything
that you need to do!

Parting is such sweet sorrow

I know that you may have become so attached to some
important files, documents, or other records that you can't
bear to part with them. But if that's the case, do they have to
stay on the top of your desk for the next 6 to 12 months? As an
alternative, why not just put them in one of the drawers in

your filing cabinet, somewhere else in your office, or send them to an off-site storage facility? This way, you can have the best of both worlds. If you need the materials somewhere down the road, you know where to find them. And with the passage of time, they may become less important and you can throw them away at that time.

Working with Your Keeper Pile

After you've gone through all the stuff on your desk and have put the papers and documents you need to keep in a keeper pile, it's time to take a moment and see what it is that you've collected. As you go through the pile, you'll find that you have some work to do. So when you discover that you've got to write a letter, memo, or fax; work on a presentation or proposal; or make a telephone call, note this to-do item on your Master List. (In Part II, you'll learn how to use your Master List.)

After you've made this entry on your Master List, you can either file the paper or throw it away. The decision's yours. You'll also come across papers, documents, and other information that you want to keep. Put these things in properly labeled file folders and then put the folders in a filing cabinet.

And should you come across something that belongs to someone else, pass it on to its owner and get it off your desk.

There are three things to remember when you handle a piece of paper:

- When there's work to do, note it on your Master List.
- If you need to keep a piece of paper, file it away.
- If you don't need to keep a piece of paper, throw it away.

As you're going through your keeper pile, you may find some miscellaneous papers that you need to keep for a short period of time. Afterwards, you can throw them away or put them in a more permanent file. A "things to-do" file is a great place to store these temporary papers.

To create a things-to-do file, just take a plain manila folder and write "things to-do" across the top. Isn't that easy?

If you have work to do regarding a piece of paper, never place it inside your things-to-do file, or any other file for that matter, without first noting it on your Master List (see Part II for more info on Master Lists). If you put the paper away, you may forget about it.

Getting Rid of Sticky Notes

I don't know about you, but most of the business people I've met love to write messages to themselves on sticky notes and other tiny pieces of paper and stick them to the wall, their computer monitors, their phones, or almost anything else they might adhere to. They think that because they can see all of these notes, or reminders, of things to do that they'll remember to do them. But it just doesn't work out that way because although they see the note, it probably won't motivate them to make the call, write the letter, or do whatever else it's supposed to remind them to do.

If you have something to do, note it on your Master List

If you're writing something down as a reminder on a little piece of paper or on a sticky note, you'll never remember to do it. Instead, add the item to your Master List. (It's much easier to scan a list of 25 items than to look at 25 separate sticky notes sticking to the wall.)

When you write something down, use big pieces of paper

If you've got to write something down, use a big piece of paper. Little pieces of paper just get lost. And, with a big piece of paper, you've got a lot more space on which to write.

Don't forget to file your notes

If you're going to take detailed notes of your telephone conversations and meetings, you should file them in the appropriate place — inside a file folder. This way, you'll be able to find them when you need them.

Cleaning Up the Mess Inside Your Desk

You can't stop just yet. You've done a great job of getting rid of the clutter that's been on the top of your desk, but you're not quite finished. You've got to go through the drawers, the big ones and the little ones, in your desk. (If you're tired or exhausted, you don't have to do it this very moment. Maybe you can get to it tomorrow or the next day when your energy has returned.)

After you get started, you'll find that at least 80 percent of the papers that you've stuffed in these drawers can be tossed. That's because your working papers and to-do items have been sitting in piles on the top of your desk. (If you've still got the files that belonged to the person who had the desk before you did, and you've had the desk for two years, it's time to throw those old files away.) If you want to keep some papers and the file folder is beat up, make a new folder.

Cleaning Out Your Briefcase

Are you one of those people who keep their briefcases filled with work, reading materials, and other things that they take home each night and never look at? If so, let's empty its contents and see what you've got in there. If there's actual work to do, note it on your Master List and plan to do it during regular business hours. If you need to keep something, file it away. The rest should be pitched.

Organizing Reading Material

Are you one of those people who subscribes to two or three daily newspapers, several weekly, bi-weekly, and monthly magazines, as well as every one of your industry's trade journals? If you're like most people, you don't have enough time to read even a small fraction of this material, and it's so voluminous that if you were to take the time to read it, there wouldn't be any time left for your meetings and telephone calls, let alone your *real* work.

So what do you do with all of this material? You stick it in a "reading" pile and never look at it again. Interestingly enough, the world doesn't come to an end simply because you don't read all the things that cross your desk. Somehow, you get along very well without the information you didn't know you were missing. Here are some thoughts on coping with all of this reading material:

- If you've got newspapers that are more than a few days old, throw them away. The news is already old and stale.

- If your magazines are more than a week or two old (if the magazine's a monthly, two months old), get rid of them, too.

- If you have publications that you don't ever read, cancel the subscriptions.

Setting Up a Reading File

As an alternative to having stacks of newspapers, magazines, and trade journals lying around, why don't you set up a reading file for yourself?

When you receive a magazine, quickly skim the table of contents, and if you see an article that you think may be of interest, rip the pages out of the magazine and throw the rest of it away. Then put the article in a reading file that you can take with you on your next business trip.

If you don't want to rip up the magazine, just circle the page number of the article you want to read in the table of contents or put a sticky note on the page where the article starts.

To get the information you want out of your daily newspaper, scan the paper very quickly. When you find an article that's of interest, rip out the page, put the article in a reading file, and recycle the newspaper.

Always read with a pen in your hand. Whenever you're reading anything — a letter, report, memo, newspaper, or magazine, always have a pen nearby so that you can circle or highlight any words, sentences, or phrases that you find of interest. You should also write any thoughts, comments, or questions that you may have in the margins.

Filing Your Papers

After you've gone through all the junk and clutter that's been on the top of your desk, and thrown away *all* the stuff you no longer need, you've got to find a place to store the things you want to keep. It's my suggestion that you put your important papers and records in properly labeled file folders, and put the folders inside your file drawer. This way, you can find the things you need — without having to tear the office apart — whenever you need them. Here are some tips.

Use file folders

Instead of leaving letters, memos, reports, and other papers lying on the top of your desk, put them in file folders. You may even remember having seen manila file folders in a previous life.

Use new folders

How's this for a *new* idea: Use new file folders. Don't try to pinch pennies by reusing old, beat-up file folders, ones that only cost a nickel. Use a new one. And when your old folders become beat up, dog-eared, and dirty, replace them.

Collate your file folders

Most folders come with file tabs in three separate positions — left, center, and right. If you collate your files, it will be much easier for you to see the labels on your folders because you can see three labels at once.

If you have a lot of alphabetical files, make the tabs mean something to you. This works best if you use files that have tabs in three positions: left, center, and right. When you set up your filing system in this manner, it makes pulling files from the drawer and refiling them much easier: Put the letters of the alphabet on the file tabs in this order:

Left	Center	Right
A	B	C
D	E	F
G	H, I	J
K	L	M
N	O	P, Q
R	S	T
U, V	W	X, Y, Z

Label your files

How will you ever know what's inside your file if you don't write a label for it?

 Don't write the label on the front of the file; write it on the tab so that when it's in the file drawer, you can read it.

Write your file labels by hand

You probably think that gummed labels look very nice, pretty, and professional. But it's a very time consuming and expensive process to type labels, especially when you've got to do it with a typewriter, because it's not easy to type a single label with a computer. So it's my suggestion that you keep a supply of file folders in your desk drawer, and when you need one, just pull it out and write the label with a fine-tipped pen (pencils smudge and soon become illegible). It's done in a matter of seconds.

 If you *do* want typed labels, get a Seiko Smart Label Printer PRO. The SLP Printer PRO attaches to the serial port of your computer and prints labels from a roll, one at a time, instead of from a sheet. I use mine every day and find that it's a great productivity-improvement tool. **Seiko Smart Label Printer PRO.** Seiko Instruments USA Inc., 1130 Ringwood Court, San Jose, CA 95131, 800-888-0817.

File labels should read like the telephone directory

When you're writing labels for the names of people, they should be written just like you see it in the telephone directory: Last Name, First Name, Middle Initial.

Color code your files

To make locating your files easier, try color coding your files. You can do this in one of several ways. Use different colored pens, or write the file's name on the tab and use a colored highlighter to color code the folder. (I think this method is much easier than using the gummed file labels with the colored strips across the top.)

Get rid of your hanging folders

Many people use hanging folders to keep their manila folders from falling over. In theory, this system is okay, but in practice, it just doesn't work because the hanging folders themselves can take up as much as a third of the space in an empty drawer. If you find that your file drawers are filled beyond capacity, get rid of the hanging folders and replace them with expandable file pockets.

Use expandable file pockets

As an alternative to these hanging folders, use expandable file pockets (also called accordion files). You'll find that the pockets that expand to 3 inches will fill most of your needs. You put the file folders inside the file pockets and then put the pockets into your file drawers. They stand up all by themselves.

Organize your files

After you've put your important papers in the manila folders, you should put the manila folders inside the expandable file pockets. But don't just put them in haphazardly. Think about how you use your files. Files that belong together should be put in the same file pocket, and files that you look at or review frequently should be in the front of the file pocket.

Put the file pockets in your desk's file drawer

The last step in the process is to put the file pockets inside the
file drawer of your desk. Files that you use all the time should
be placed at the front of the drawer so that they're easy to get
to. Files you use less frequently can be placed behind them.
Other files that you need to keep, but won't look at very often,
should be placed in the drawers of your credenza, in other
filing cabinets in the office, or in permanent off-site storage.

 When you place the file pockets inside your desk file drawer,
turn them so that they face you instead of having them face
straight back.

 Work from your file folders. After you set up your filing
system, you should get into the habit of working from your
files. This way, you will always have the information you need
at your fingertips and won't have to rely on your memory.

Cleaning Up Your Hard Drive

Cleaning off the top of the desk and the inside of the file
drawers is the first part of the job. But there's another filing
cabinet that you can't forget to clean up. It's the hard drive on
your computer. And I'm sure there's a lot of old stuff inside
your computer that you can get rid of. (If you don't use a
computer, you can skip these next few pages and learn how to
create an effective follow-up system in Part II.)

A hard drive is nothing more than an electronic filing cabinet.
And no matter how large a hard drive you've got, if you
continue to add more and more files and computer programs
without deleting the ones you no longer need or use, the drive,
like the file drawers in your office, will eventually become
stuffed beyond capacity. Until you actually start getting rid of
your old computer files and unused programs, you won't
realize how much space you're wasting.

Tips for Mac users

If you're a Windows user, skip to the next section.

It's easy to delete files on a Mac. Just select the file or folders
you don't want to keep and drag them to the Trash. Then
choose the Empty Trash command from the Special menu.

To determine which files you ought to delete, view a given folder by date. The files within the folder will appear in order from newest to oldest. Chances are, you'll want to trash the oldest files.

Tips for DOS/Windows users

The next few paragraphs will help DOS and Windows users get rid of unneeded files on their hard drives.

Delete your automatic backup files

When cleaning up your hard drive, the first thing you should do is delete your automatic backup files. Many programs, such as your word processor and spreadsheet, have a feature that automatically backs up a file. You can recognize this type of file because it has the extension .BK! or .BAK.

This is how an automatic backup file is created. Let's say you create a document — a letter to a friend — whose file name is C:\LETTER. A little while later, you decide to make a change to the letter, so you open the file, make your changes, and then save it. This is what your automatic backup program did. The original version of C:\LETTER becomes C:\LETTER.BAK, and the revised version becomes C:\LETTER.

You can always tell which version of a file is older by looking at the date and time it was last saved.

If you've been writing a lot of letters, memos, presentations, and reports, and you have been using your programs' automatic backup features, you may have a lot of backup files that are taking up a great deal of valuable space on your hard drive. It's very easy to get rid of your backup files. First, open your File Manager and select a directory. All the files within the directory will be displayed. Then sort the files in the directory by extension.

In the Windows File Manager, select View and then Sort by Type, and the directory is sorted by the type of file.

Now, scroll through the list of files for the ones that have the *.BAK extension. You can then delete the files one at a time. Or, if you hold down the Shift key while clicking your mouse, you can select a group of files and delete them all at once.

To select files that are not next to each other, hold down the Ctrl button while you select the individual files with your mouse.

Delete unneeded files

After you get rid of your backup files, you should delete old files that you no longer need. And if you're like me, I'm sure you've got plenty of them. You can delete files in one of two ways — from the File Manager or from within the program that created the file, such as your word processor.

Select a directory and browse through the files, one at a time. If you no longer need a file, delete it. If you're not sure at this particular moment whether or not you should keep a specific file, create an archive directory where you can store these old files and get them out of the way. At a future time, you can go in and delete the files you no longer need.

Find a retirement home for your old computer files

If you have files that you want to keep on your hard drive but don't need to access very often, create a permanent archive directory (a *folder* on a Mac) where you can move them just to get them out of the way.

Copy unneeded files to floppy disks

If you want to keep specific files but don't need to store them on your hard drive, then copy the files to a floppy disk and keep it in a safe place.

When you save files onto a floppy disk, be sure to write a label for the floppy disk that properly describes each of the files. Then print a hard copy of the disk's directories and subdirectories, fold the piece of paper until it's about the same size as the disk, and use a rubber band to keep it securely attached. Now you'll always know what files are on the disk — even if you don't look at it for a year. And if you want to make some additional notations as to the nature of these files, you can write them on the piece of paper.

Get rid of someone else's old files

A few pages ago, I asked whether you were sitting at a desk that had the previous occupant's files in the file drawers. To ask a question that goes a bit deeper, are you sitting at the previous occupant's computer, and are that person's computer files still on the hard drive?

If so, it's time to go through them and delete the ones you don't need. Here are some tips on how to do some hard drive house cleaning:

- Check the dates of the files to determine how old they are. Make sure that you're looking at *data* files and not your program or system files. If you delete any program or system files, you'll be in big trouble.

- Before you delete any files, you should view them — one by one — to determine whether there is anything important in the files. If you find an important file, you have two options: (1) print it out, file the hard copy away, and delete the file, or (2) if you want to keep the computer file, move it to one of the directories you've created. If there's nothing of importance in the file, delete it.

- If you want to keep some or all of the files (just to be sure that you don't get rid of something important), you can leave them alone for the time being and make a note that some time in the future the files should be purged. Or you can save the files to a floppy disk, put it in a safe place, and get the files off your hard drive.

Which do you want: the paper copy or the computer file?

If you have printouts of your computer files, do you need to keep both the hard copy and the computer file? Keeping both is often redundant. So would you rather recycle the papers or delete the computer file?

 Copy the computer file onto a floppy disk, label it appropriately, and delete it from your hard drive. Then put the disk into the proper file and recycle the paper copy.

Delete your old computer programs

How many programs do you have on your computer that you no longer use? Do you still have the DOS version of a program even though you've been using the Windows version for years? Have you replaced one program with a better one but never got around to removing the old one? And what about the software that you tried for a few days or weeks and then you decided that you didn't like it and never used it again? If you answered "yes" to any of these questions, it's time to do some hard drive house cleaning.

- On a Mac, simply drag old programs to the Trash and choose the Empty Trash command from the Special menu.

- Deleting a DOS program is easy because all you have to do is open the File Manager, go to the directory that contains the program's files, mark the files, and press the Delete key.

- Deleting a Windows program can be tricky because Windows programs are a lot more complicated than DOS programs. (The first time I tried to delete a Windows program, I just deleted the program's icon in the Program Manager. Little did I know that I had only deleted the symbol that turned the program on. The program files were still on my hard drive.)

Uninstall your Windows programs

I wouldn't recommend that you try to delete any of the specific lines from the WIN.INI file, or even the *.INI files, because the task can be rather tricky and complicated, especially if you're not an experienced computer user. So instead of trying to delete all these program files, icons, and lines of *.INI text yourself — and possibly delete something that you shouldn't — you can use a utility program that's designed to uninstall your unused Windows programs. Here are two programs that will do it for you:

- **UnInstaller.** MicroHelp, Inc., 439 Shallowford Industrial Parkway, Marietta, GA 30066, 800-922-3383.

- **Clean Sweep.** Quarterdeck Office Systems, Inc., 150 Pico Boulevard, Santa Monica, CA 90405, 310-392-9851.

Organize Your Hard Drive

One of the biggest problems everyone has in working within the DOS and Windows operating environment comes from the system's inability to accept file names that mean something. With DOS, you're limited to an eight-character file name with a three-character extension.

A note for Mac users: You Mac people have it easy. You don't have to worry about file name extensions or eight-character file name limitations. In addition, creating a new folder (or directory, in old-fashioned DOS-speak) is as easy as choosing the New Folder command from the File menu in the Finder. Throughout the rest of this section, I use DOS/Windows terminology, but you can still pick up a few helpful tips (and see how most of the world has to wrestle with an operating system that's somewhat less elegant than the Mac's). Just remember that a directory is the same as a folder, and most of this section will make sense to you.

A hard drive is an electronic filing cabinet

From my perspective, a hard drive is nothing more than an electronic filing cabinet, and I would like to begin by telling you some of the things that you shouldn't do, because if you don't organize your computer files, you'll eventually be working in chaos.

Don't put all of your files in your root (C:\) directory

In no time at all, you'll have so many files that you won't know what files are there or which programs they belong to.

Don't store your document files with your program files

Don't store your document files in the same directory as your operating system or program files such as WordPerfect, Lotus 1-2-3, Quicken, ACT!, and so on. If you store files in this manner, you're flirting with disaster. It's too easy to accidentally delete a program or system file because you thought it was an old letter or memo you no longer needed. (How did you know that a file with a *.BAT, *.COM, *.EXE, or *.DLL extension was important?) After you delete such a file, you'll find that your word processor or even your computer won't run — and you won't have the slightest idea why.

Don't make your root directory (C:\) your default directory

The *default* directory is the directory in which every file is automatically saved. Your root directory should be reserved for your program and working file directories and the handful of files that are needed to make your computer run, like the CONFIG.SYS and AUTOEXEC.BAT files. (If you want to know more about AUTOEXEC.BAT and CONFIG.SYS files, pick up a copy of the latest edition of *DOS For Dummies*.)

Set up separate directories

I'm also not a big fan of using three-character extensions as a method of trying to identify different types of files. For example, many people use extensions such as .DOC for documents, .PRO for proposals, .MEM for memo, and so on. But they're doing this because they've *dumped* everything into one directory.

I think it makes much more sense to set up separate directories and subdirectories that can be used to store similar types of information. When you set up your directories in a logical, systematic manner, you'll save yourself hours of time in the future.

If, for example, you've got a big client who generates a lot of correspondence, set up a separate directory for this person or firm and don't mix these files with any other files. Give the directory a name like BIG_CLNT. Now, you'll probably have different kinds of files for this client, so you should have additional directories, that is, subdirectories, named: LETTERS, PROPOSAL, SPRD_SHT, or any other topic or category that you feel would be appropriate.

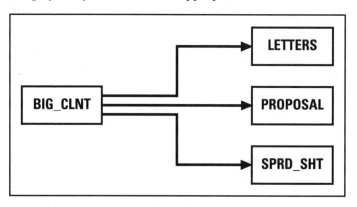

Give your files a name that means something. Don't name your files by the creation date. How will you know what's in a file with a name like: C:\LETTERS\01-07.DOC? Wouldn't it make more sense to give it a name like C:\LETTERS\SALESCON for a document that was written concerning a sales contract? Or, if you have different versions of the contract, start numbering them by using the three-character extension: SALESCON.1,

SALESCON.2. With this method of organizing and naming your directories and files, you'll be able to locate your files in a matter of moments.

To continue with the preceding example, if you send correspondence to several people on a regular basis, why not create separate sub-subdirectories to store their correspondence. As shown in the following figure, if you regularly send letters to John, Sue, and Bill, create separate subdirectories under the LETTERS subdirectory. This way, you can keep all your correspondence organized.

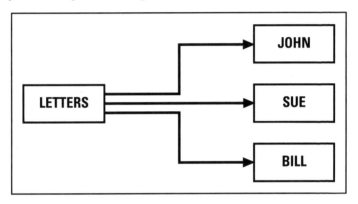

 When a directory begins to get too large — more than 30 or 40 files — start looking for files that relate to each other or that can be grouped together. Then create a new subdirectory and move them into it. This way, it's easy to manage your files.

Cleaning Up at the End of the Day

Before you go home at the end of the day, you should spend a few minutes to clean up your desk. Put the papers you need to keep in the appropriate files, and put the files back into the file drawer. Anything you don't need should be thrown away. Go through your stack of mail, listen to your voice-mail messages, and scan your e-mail to see what items of business need to be added to your Master List. Take a few moments to review your Master List so that you can select your most important work, and then plan to do it when you arrive tomorrow morning.

Go through all the things that have accumulated on your desk during the day — at the end of the day — and you'll find that it's relatively easy to stay organized. If you've been busy for several days and things have backed up and stacked up on you, just stop cold and take a few minutes to get your desk cleaned up and organized. In no time at all, you'll be back to work.

After you get organized, you're going to find that you absolutely love it. You'll find that you're able to do a better job of staying on top of your important work, tasks, and projects. You'll feel that you've got much more control over your work. And when you leave the office at the end of the day, you'll pat yourself on the back and congratulate yourself for a job well done.

Your goal is to complete as much work as possible during normal business hours. When you go home at the end of the day, you've earned the right to relax and spend some quiet time with your family, your friends, and yourself.

Part II

Working with Your Master List

*W*hat does the top of your desk look like? Do you still have piles of stuff everywhere? (If so, you should read this part of the book and then read Part I, if you haven't done so already, and then get yourself organized.) Well, if you're trying to stay on top of all of your unfinished work, tasks, projects, and telephone calls — and you're doing it by leaving everything out on the top of your desk — then you're flirting with disaster. It's just impossible to keep on top of everything, or anything, when your office looks as if a tornado has gone through it. Important things get lost, misplaced, or are soon forgotten, and at the very least it takes a lot of time — wasted time — to find that letter, memo, file, or report when you need it. And why did you begin to look for it in the first place? Because your boss just asked for it, and he or she is standing at your doorway; or someone just called and is waiting patiently, or impatiently, on hold while you frantically search through the stacks of papers on your desk.

You may not be aware of this fact, but most people waste at least an hour each day looking for papers that are lost on the top of their desks. By getting organized, you can convert the time that's usually wasted during the course of a normal business day into time that can be used more productively and efficiently.

With piles of papers everywhere it does become very difficult, if not impossible, to stay on top of the important things in your life.

The next few pages are meant to convince you that using piles of paper is an inefficient follow-up system. After I get you to agree that you need to change your evil ways, I'll show you how a Master List is a better follow-up system.

Oh, Where Did I Put My Calendar?

I know that you've never given this much thought, but many of the things that remain on the top of the desk are left out as reminders of things to do. We think that by seeing a piece of unfinished business, it will remind us to write that letter or

make that call, and we'll do it. In theory, this may sound great; in practice, it just doesn't work! Yes, you do get things done, and you often, but not always, meet your deadlines, but you're paying a price: It takes a lot more effort and exertion on your part to get the work done, usually because you start working on a project when there's no lead-time left. So your stress level is higher than it should be, and I would venture to say that the quality of your work isn't always at the highest level that you're capable of producing.

One of the main causes of efficiency problems is the piles themselves. The piles of papers are supposed to remind a person of the tasks he or she is supposed to do, but that person never gets to these tasks until the last minute because the papers were put aside and forgotten within the piles. And the person doesn't start work on the task or project until someone calls to ask, "Where is it?" Now this person has to drop everything to do something that's been sitting around for a month.

I'll get to it later . . .

Do you ever go through your in-box and look at the pile of letters, memos, and reports that have accumulated and just put them aside in an "I'll get to it later" pile? Well, you're not alone because almost everybody else is doing it too. But when you put things aside in this manner, you're going to create problems for yourself because once you get into the habit of leaving piles of paper everywhere, too many things end up in the "I'll get to it later" pile. And later never comes.

Over the years, I've had many people say to me, "I put things aside, and if I don't get a follow-up call or additional correspondence, I'll eventually throw it away." This system may be an easy way to get through the day, but it isn't necessarily the best way to take control of the things that are going on in your business life, and it certainly isn't an efficient way to manage all the papers that come cross your desk. When you just put things aside, you're putting yourself in the position of waiting for things to happen, and then you're forced to react to them. You're no longer making your own decisions, and you've lost control of your daily business affairs.

But I Know Where Everything Is

Now I know you're going to tell me that you know where everything is, and I'm sure that you do, but the question isn't: "Do you know where everything is?" The real question is: "Do you know what work, tasks, and projects you have to do, and when you have to do them?"

- Whom do you have to call?

- From whom are you awaiting a telephone call?

- To whom are you supposed to be sending a letter, memo, presentation, proposal, or other piece of information?

- Who is supposed to be sending you a letter, memo, presentation, proposal, or other piece of information?

The answer to these questions has nothing to do with whether or not you know that a particular piece of paper is sitting three inches from the top of one pile, or two inches from the bottom of another.

The fact that you *think* you know where something is has nothing to do with your ability to get your work done, get it done on time, or even done well. Many times the work will remain undone until someone asks for it, and it's at this time that you must drop everything so you can complete a task that should have been done days ago. Now you have another fire to put out, your whole day is going up in smoke, and you don't even realize that you're guilty of arson.

So instead of leaving things out in piles, you'll find that you can be much more efficient and productive when you keep a list of all of your tasks, projects, and other items of business on what I call a *Master List,* which is a things-to-do list that's written on a large piece of paper. By writing everything down on your Master List, you give yourself the ability to maintain total control over everything that's going on in both your business and your personal life.

An Efficient Follow-Up System Is the Key to Being Successful

I know that you work hard, that you put in a lot of hours on the job, and that you're dedicated to your company. But hard work and dedication can only take you so far, and after a while there just aren't any more hours left in the work day or the work week. So if you want to become more efficient and effective; improve your ability to stay on top of all of the unfinished work, tasks, projects, and correspondence; and be able to do your work faster and better, then all you've got to do is improve your follow-up systems. Here are some of the things that an efficient follow-up system will do for you:

- It will help you get your work done well and on time.

- It will help you improve the quality of your work.

- It will give you the opportunity to start your important projects while you've got plenty of lead time.

- It will help you remember who you're supposed to call and when you're supposed to call.

- It will give you complete control of your business affairs.

- You will be able to stay on top of the work you've delegated to others.

- It will enable you to compress the amount of time it takes to make decisions.

- You won't have to spend so much time putting out fires because fewer fires will start.

- It will give you the ability to juggle lots of balls all at once — without dropping any of them — thus avoiding the time-consuming and costly process of dealing with emergencies that easily could have been avoided.

- You will have complete control over your schedule, your day, and yourself.

- At the end of the day you will be able to say to yourself, "I *really* got a lot done today."

- You will be able to get a good night's sleep.

- You will get to stay home on the weekends.

- You will have more time to spend with your friends and family, doing the things that you enjoy.

With an effective follow-up system, things just don't slip through the cracks. You're able to stay on top of your most important work, tasks, and projects. You get your work done on time, you do it well, and you make it home for dinner.

Now that you're aware of the importance of having a good and thorough follow-up system, sit back and relax as you read the next few pages because I'm going to explain how easy it is to set up an efficient follow-up system. I start by showing you how to make a Master List of all your things to do. In Part III, I explain how to get the most out of your daily planner. And in Part IV, you'll learn how easy it is to put your daily planner inside your computer with the ACT! contact-management program.

What Is a Master List?

The basic concept behind using a Master List is that by writing everything down in an orderly, meticulous way, you can do a better job of staying on top of all of your unfinished work, tasks, projects, and correspondence. When you put things down on paper, you don't have to remember as many things.

Now, I know that you've been writing things down for years; you just haven't been doing it methodically. You've been writing names, addresses, and phone numbers on Post-It Notes and sticking them on the wall; you've been keeping to-do lists on the backs of envelopes; and you've been scribbling notes to yourself on any piece of paper that you can get your hands on. So yes, you've been in the habit of writing things down, but the manner in which you've been doing it isn't a very efficient or effective way of staying on top of all of your unfinished work. By using a Master List to keep an itemized inventory of your unfinished work, you will have an organized and systematic format for maintaining control of your workload and your workday.

Shouldn't I Handle a Piece of Paper Only Once?

I know that you've heard the old adage, "You should handle a piece of paper only once," but that advice just doesn't work in the high-pressure business world of the 90s. And besides, we're not only dealing with paper because we've got voice mail, e-mail, and all kinds of computer files. So you shouldn't be concerned if you handle a piece of paper once, twice, or a dozen times. The number of times you handle a piece of paper isn't important; what *is* important is that you make a decision about what you're going to do with that piece of paper.

When something crosses your desk, make a decision — *now* — instead of waiting to see what happens next. If there's work to do, it should be noted on your Master List. If you need to keep that piece of paper, file it away. And if you don't need it any longer, pass it on to someone else, put it in the recycling bin, or throw it away.

You shouldn't keep unneeded or unnecessary papers in a pile on the top of your desk for the next six months.

Getting the Most out of Your Master List

Over the next several pages, I provide advice on setting up and using a Master List. Much of the information might sound like common sense, but you'd be surprised how many people don't practice the simple techniques illustrated here. So read it carefully.

Use a big piece of paper

It's my suggestion that you keep your Master List on a big piece of paper. That way, you've got 25 lines on a page with which to list your projects, tasks, and the other items of business that you must do or follow up on. And because you're using a big piece of paper instead of a Post-It Note or the back of an envelope, you've got enough space to not only

include information such as names and phone numbers, but you can also include things like the purpose of a phone call and any other pertinent information. If necessary, you can even write this additional information on a second or a third line.

Don't skip lines. When you're adding items of business to your Master List, make it a point to use every line so that you can get 25 items listed on a page instead of 12.

Write everything down

The key to making your Master List work for you is to make sure that you write everything down. The more tasks, projects, calls, and other to-do items that you put down on paper, the greater your ability to control the events that are taking place during the workday.

Add additional pages to your Master List

When you've used up all of the lines on the first page, don't be afraid to start a second one. It's common for most people to have a Master List that's one or two pages in length.

Cross off completed tasks

When you've completed a task, project, or other item of business, give yourself the pleasure of crossing it off your list. Don't just place a check mark in the margin; it's not gratifying enough. You should draw a line through it instead.

Transfer unfinished items and consolidate the pages of your Master List

The key to making your Master List work for you is to transfer and consolidate the unfinished items of business from the older pages to the newest ones. As a general rule, when 50 percent of the items on a particular page have been completed, transfer the unfinished items — one at a time — to the newest page, and cross them off the old page. After you've rewritten the unfinished items onto the newest page, take one last look at the old page, just to see if you've missed anything, before you dispose of it.

If you feel that it's important to keep your old Master Lists so that you've got a record of what you've accomplished, make a file and label it "Old Lists."

Get your work done

Throughout the day, you should scan the items on your Master List to determine which item of business is the most important so that you can determine which task you need to work on next. If you have a project that will take time, schedule a block of uninterrupted time on your calendar, and think of it as an appointment with the boss or your most important client — because it is!

 If you've only got 15 minutes between meetings, use this time to make or return a few phone calls. Or pick off a few of the smaller, less time-consuming tasks so that you can get rid of them.

Review your Master List before you go home

Before you go home at night, take a few minutes to review your Master List to determine which items of business are most important so that you can plan to do them tomorrow. You can also use this time as an opportunity to plan your work for the future. What do you have to do during the next few days? Next week? Next month? Your objective is to produce the highest quality work that you're capable of. When you give yourself more time to do your work, you don't have to worry about whether the first draft is good enough because you've got the time to revise. And in the end, the finished product will be great. So when you give yourself plenty of time to think about and plan your work, the work itself is much easier.

 Use your Master List as a planning tool so that you can start on all of your work, tasks, and projects while you've got sufficient lead time.

Schedule your important work for the first thing in the morning

When you schedule your work, try to tackle your most important tasks as soon as you arrive in the morning, when you're fresh, alert, and energetic. You'll be amazed at how much you can accomplish when you get into the habit of working on your most important projects early in the day, before the inevitable fires flare up.

If you give yourself the first two hours of the workday — no meetings, no phone calls, and no interruptions — you'll find that you're able to complete twice as much work, in half the time, with half the effort.

Don't rewrite your Master List every day

Some people make it a point to rewrite their things-to-do list every morning so that the most important items are at the top of the list. I think that this system is not only is a waste of time, it's a waste of effort. You're in the business of doing your work, not rewriting your lists.

You're not going to get to everything

You must also realize that you're not going to be completing each and every item on your Master List every day. Your goal is to get to your important work, do it well, and get it done on time. Your Master List is the tool that will help you stay focused on your most important tasks and projects and keep you in total control.

Unfortunately, Your Master List Can't Do Everything

The Master List is great for initially getting organized, but as you use it, you'll find that it has some shortcomings, the biggest of which is that it doesn't integrate with a calendar. Let me give you a few examples.

It's not easy to keep track of future follow-ups

Let's say you have the following item on your list: "Call Jim Smith." So you make the call and are told that Jim is not going to be in the office until Wednesday of next week. The Master List doesn't offer an efficient way to keep track of when you need to make this next call. You can write down the date on which you plan to make this call in the margin next to the original entry (or somewhere else on the line that notes the item), perhaps using a red pen. But things get more complicated when you call again and are told that Jim will be out of town for another 10 days. Now you've got to cross out the original follow-up date and replace it with a new one. Or maybe you rewrite the entire entry, or perhaps you just forget about it and hope that you'll remember to call Jim at some future date.

As you can see, the more times that you have to reschedule the follow-up date of a to-do item, the more complicated the process becomes, and your Master List gets messier and messier. A daily planner is better suited to dealing with this type of situation because you can write a person's name on the appropriate day in the calendar as a reminder that you plan to call.

How do you remember to call someone six months from now?

Another ticklish problem arises when a person asks you to follow-up in six or eight months, or, for that matter, anytime in the future. Your Master List is designed to help you stay on top of your *daily* work, not the things you may need to do in the coming months. One possible way to deal with this situation is to create a Master List that's designed solely for your long-range projects, tasks, and calls. On this Master List, you keep track of things by date. But for most people, this follow-up process can become rather cumbersome, and in the end, some important things may slip through the cracks. A daily planner can also solve this problem because you can write information down on any future date in the book.

How do you remember to start on a project six weeks from now?

Here's another problem that highlights the shortcoming of using the Master List: You've got a task or project that needs to be completed at some point in the not-so-distant future, but you don't plan to start working on it for several days, or even several weeks. Once again, a daily planner solves this problem. You just write down when you want to start on the project on a specific future date in the daily planner.

What about names, addresses, and phone numbers?

And finally, what do you do with the names, addresses, phone numbers, and notes of conversations that may have become part of your Master List? How do you keep this valuable information if you're in the habit of throwing the pages of your Master List away after the list of unfinished tasks has been transferred to another page? A daily planner gives you the ability to maintain access to this valuable information because you don't throw the old pages away. They're still in the book and are available for future reference.

Always write a person's name and phone number in your name and address book or Rolodex file so that you can find it when you need it.

It is for these and many other reasons that many people have found daily planners to be so useful when it comes to helping them take control of their daily activities and affairs. A daily planner is designed to integrate your calendar, things-to-do list, call list, meetings, and appointments into one book that can help you to stay on top of all of your unfinished work, tasks, and projects.

So what now?

Using a Master List is a great way to keep track of your daily work, but as the preceding section illustrates, you need to supplement your Master List with a daily planner, which is the topic I cover in Part III.

My Own Follow-Up System

As an author, I represent myself as my own literary agent, and in selling my books, follow-up is of prime importance. After I send a proposal, I make it a point to find out whether it has been received (I usually call within two days if I used FedEx or a within a week if I used Priority Mail). After I'm told that my proposal was received, I ask the editor how long it will be before the publisher and acquisitions people expect to get around to looking at my proposal. And after they've had a chance to look at it, how long will it take them to decide whether they want to make me an offer to publish my book.

By making these phone calls, I learn a lot about the people I'm dealing with. Some answer their own phone, and others have their calls screened by an assistant or secretary. And a small handful actually return my calls. Once I have the opportunity to speak with them, I can get a pretty good idea of their interest just by the tone of their voice as they talk to me. Some are friendly and cordial and are happy to hear from me; others are short and curt and speak to me as if I were a nuisance to them.

Based on these conversations, it is easy for me to identify both the people I should continue following up with and the people who have already decided to turn me down. Most important, by calling, I know who's interested and who isn't. And with this information I can continue to move forward. (I was once told, "If you're not being rejected, you're not trying hard enough.")

I've learned that if I contact enough people, sooner or later I will find someone who not only likes my books, but wants to buy them. That's how I sold my first four books, and that's how I sold the book you currently hold in your hands.

Part III

Using Your Daily Planner

*F*or years, people like you and me have been keeping track of our meetings, appointments, telephone calls, and unfinished work by using daily planning books — Day Timers, Day Runners, Filofaxes, and Franklin Planners. These leather bound personal organizers have been wonderful productivity-improvement tools. They've helped us set our priorities, organize and coordinate our important long-term projects, keep track of delegated work, and establish and set our goals. We also use them to jot down notes or background information about our business meetings or phone conversations, keep track of miscellaneous ideas and thoughts, and record our tax deductible or reimbursable expenses.

In addition to helping us keep track of what we need to do and when we need to do it, we use the phone book section to store the names, addresses, and phone numbers of our family, friends, customers, clients, and other important people in our lives.

We use these books not only to keep track of our daily activities, but to keep our lives in order. For some of us, these books play such an important part in our lives that we won't go anyplace without them. We even use them to carry our check books and credit cards.

It's a To-Do List, a Calendar, and a Dessert Topping

The basic concept behind the daily planner is that you use it to coordinate your list of things-to-do (your Master List), your list of people to call, and your meetings and appointments with your calendar. You're no longer writing these lists of your unfinished work, tasks, and projects on a things-to-do list; you're writing them on a specific date in the daily planning book — a date when you think you can get to them. The integration of your things-to-do list with your calendar gives you the flexibility to schedule future tasks on a date when you plan to start working on them, which in many cases will not be the date on which you wrote the items down in the book.

You Can Schedule To-Do Items on Future Days

Have you ever been given an assignment by your boss that was due in, let's say, two weeks? The boss walks into your office on Monday morning, hands you a piece of paper that outlines the project, and tells you that it has to be completed by a week from Friday. As you look at your calendar, you realize that this week is shot because of all of the other appointments and commitments you made, so you schedule this project for Tuesday of next week. And now you're assured that you can work it into your schedule and finish it without being rushed. That's what the daily planner is designed to do.

I used a guy named Jim Smith as an example in Part II, so I might as well use him again for another example here. Suppose that on Monday of this week you decide that you want to call Jim to discuss the benefits of the new product that your company is about to introduce. But in looking at your calendar, you realize that you're all booked up until Thursday, which will be your first full day in the office. So instead of writing your note to call Jim on Monday's page, you enter it in your book on the day you actually will be able to make the call, which would be Thursday.

You Have More Control of Your Scheduling

In scheduling our daily activities, we all need to have some flexibility, and with a daily planner, we've got a lot of flexibility because we're able to associate specific tasks with certain days of the week. So when someone asks you to call him or her a week from Thursday, all you have to do is write it down on Thursday's page, and it's done. And if you're asked to follow up with someone in six months, you just select a date six months in the future, write down the person's name and the purpose or nature of the call on that page, and when that date arrives, six months from now, you'll find that person's name with your note to give him or her a call.

A daily planner also gives you flexibility in planning your schedule and work flow. With a Master List, you're always looking at a list of everything you need to do — things that need to be done today, as well as those tasks that need to be done in the future. When you're using a daily planner, you don't need to list all of your to-dos, calls, and other tasks on a single day. You can spread them out so that you do some of the work today, some tomorrow, and the rest on the following day. And if you find that you're not going to be able to get to certain tasks because of your other commitments, you can write down those tasks on days on which you know that you can get to them.

When you use your daily planner, instead of a piece of paper, to list all of the tasks you need to complete, the projects you need to begin working on, the letters or memos you've got to write, and the other items of business you ought to follow up on, then you have much more control of your day. You have control because you're able to associate an unfinished task or other item of business with a specific date on the calendar.

Making Your Daily Planner Work for You

If you've been keeping track of all of your unfinished work, tasks, calls, and projects on a Master List, the first thing you'll have to do is transfer the items to the pages of your daily planner. If you haven't been keeping track of things with a Master List, it's about time you started writing everything down and getting yourself organized. So if you haven't done so already, please read Part I (getting your office cleaned up) and Part II (developing a Master List).

Transfer your to-do items to your daily planner

As you review your Master List, ask yourself when you plan to get to each specific task and write it down on the day you expect to be able to get to it, start it, or complete it. Don't write things down on a day when you already know that you're going to be tied up in meetings or out of town. As you transfer each item to your daily planner, draw a line through it to ensure that you don't miss anything. When each item on your Master List has been transferred, you can throw the list away.

Add new items of business to your daily planner

Throughout the day, new items of business will come up, and they should be entered immediately in your book on the day that you plan to do them. Just because you were assigned a project this morning doesn't mean that it has to be entered on today's page of your daily planner. Maybe it should be entered on tomorrow's page, or one day next week. By writing things down immediately, they won't become buried in a pile and easily lost or forgotten.

Cross off completed items of business

As you complete a task or project, you should draw a line through it. (A check just isn't gratifying enough.) The line is your way of knowing that the task was in fact completed.

Move each unfinished piece of business to a future day, one item at a time

The single most important part of keeping your daily planner up to date comes when you move the unfinished work from one day to another. Many times, when a day has ended, a person just turns the page of his or her daily planner without checking to make sure that everything that had been entered on that day had actually been done. In most cases, there are at least one or two items, sometimes many more, that remain undone. Because the person hasn't moved these items forward, he or she must continually flip through the daily planner to see which items of business weren't completed. This method of organization guarantees that something will slip through the cracks.

Draw a line through each item as you transfer it and then draw a big X across the page

To guarantee that nothing slips through the cracks, at the end of each day, go through the to-do items, one at a time, and move them to a future day. You can move them to tomorrow, later in the week, or some other date in the future. After you move each item, you should draw a line through it, and when all of the items have been moved, you should draw a big **X** across the page. By drawing a line from one corner of the page to the other, you know that everything on that page has either been completed or moved forward. And when you see that **X**, you know that you never have to refer to that page again.

Use a pencil to schedule appointments

When you schedule your meetings or appointments, write them into your daily planner with a pencil because half of all the appointments that you schedule will be rescheduled or postponed. By using a pencil, you can erase the meeting from your daily planner. If you use a pen, you have to scratch it out.

Write your to-do and call items with a pen

Use a pen to write your to-do items and follow-ups into your book. Pencils tend to smudge, and since you won't be erasing these items, you'll have a more permanent record of the things that you did or need to do.

Write your phone numbers in your Rolodex file or in your name and address book

If you're in the habit of writing people's names, phone numbers, or other information on the pages of your daily planner, you must transfer that information to your name and address book, Rolodex file, or database file. Otherwise, you may not be able to find a piece of information when you need it, or at the very least, it won't be at your fingertips. Should you need this information after the end of the current calendar year, when you're using a new daily planner, you may never be able to locate that information again.

Block out vacation time for yourself

Most of us are spending too many hours at the office and not enough time with our family and friends. So go through your daily planner and decide when you want to take a vacation. If you don't block out time for yourself, there won't be any.

At the beginning of each year, a friend of mine, who is the vice-chairman and chief financial officer of a Fortune 500 company and on the board of directors of several public companies, asks for a list of all the various meetings that he is expected to attend during the coming year. After he enters these meetings into his daily planner, he then decides when he wants to take his vacations and also enters those dates. He knows that if he doesn't block out some time for himself, there won't be any.

Add birthdays and anniversaries

Add the birthdays and anniversaries of your family, friends, relatives, and important customers or clients to your daily planner so that you'll remember to send a card, buy a present, or invite them out to celebrate that special day.

Make the entry into your daily planner at least two weeks in advance of that special day so that you'll have plenty of time to go out and buy a card or gift.

Daily Planners Do Have Limitations

You will find that there are some limitations to using a daily planner, based on the simple fact that you're using a pencil and paper. I'm going to point out these shortcomings now, because in the next chapter, I'm going to explain why I think you should replace your paper-based personal organizer with a computerized contact manager.

Today, it's easy to harness the power of your computer to help you stay on top of every task and project that crosses your desk. With a computerized contact manager, it's no longer necessary to write and rewrite the same information over and over again. You can spend your time doing your work, instead of planning to do your work. The rest of this section shows some examples of what I mean.

It's not easy to keep your to-do list up to date

As I've described previously, it takes a lot of work to keep a list of things to-do up to date. We meticulously write down the names of various tasks, projects, or other items of business that need to be done on a specific day's page in our daily planning book. But if that item isn't done on the day it was entered, it must be moved to a future day. And if it's not moved, we run the risk of forgetting about it.

A computerized contact manager solves this problem because an unfinished task is automatically moved forward at the beginning of each day.

Moving or changing to-do items can be a lot of work

I'll use the Jim Smith example again. Suppose that you have a to-do item that says "Call Jim Smith to set up a luncheon appointment." In all likelihood, you'll have to move this item around several times before you're able to schedule the appointment. On Monday, you call and learn that he's out until Friday. When you call on Friday, you're told that he's in meetings all day and won't be in the office again until the following Thursday. And when you call on Thursday, you finally get through and set up your luncheon meeting for the following Wednesday.

Now look at what you did physically to schedule this appointment. First, you wrote down the item: "Call Jim Smith to set up luncheon appointment." Then you wrote it a second time when you moved it to Friday, and you wrote it a third time when you moved it to the following Thursday. When you scheduled the luncheon appointment for Wednesday, you wrote the item a fourth time as you entered the luncheon appointment on your calendar.

And if you weren't in the habit of moving items of business from one page to another in your daily planner, it's quite likely that you would never have gotten around to scheduling the appointment in the first place because you would have forgotten about it. (This is a perfect example of how easy it is for a person to lose track of things by not continually writing things down.)

A computerized contact manager, on the other hand, can automate this task for you. For starters, you only have to enter the item once on your to-do list. Thereafter, you only have to change the date. When you were told on Monday that Jim was out until Friday, you just clicked on the pop-up calendar and double-clicked on Friday's date; the item was moved electronically. When you called on Friday and were told that he was out until Thursday, you clicked on the pop-up calendar again and then double-clicked on Thursday's date; the to-do item was once again moved electronically.

When you turned on your computer on Thursday morning, the item that said "Call Jim Smith to set up luncheon appointment" was at the top of your list of things to do. And when you spoke to Jim on Thursday and scheduled the luncheon appointment for Wednesday, all you had to do was change the to-do item to a meeting, change the date to Wednesday, and select the time.

With a contact manager, it's easy to move items from your to-do list to your appointment calendar and back again because it's all done electronically. With just a few clicks of the mouse, you have complete control of everything that's going on in your business life.

Do you like to carry your calendar around with you?

Many people have more than one calendar. They keep a calendar on the desk and also carry a pocket calendar with them when they travel or are out of the office. And secretaries or administrative assistants often keep a third calendar so that additional appointments can be scheduled while people are away from the office. But when people keep more than one calendar, eventually they're going to experience scheduling problems.

He who has two calendars never knows his true appointment schedule. (And the same goes for the "Shes" out there.)

A computerized calendar guarantees that you'll always have a true picture of your daily activities — appointments, calls, and to-dos — because it's always up to date. Your assistant can have a printed copy of it on his or her desk, and when you leave the office, you take a printed copy with you. If your assistant has access to your computer, he or she can make changes to your calendar. If you're on a network, your assistant can access your calendar from another computer.

It takes a lot of effort to keep track of the important people in your life

In today's fast-paced world, it's not easy to keep a person's vital information up to date. Everyone has a direct phone number and fax number. Then there's a number for the beeper, the car phone, mobile telephone, and home phone. To make this record keeping more complicated, most people will probably change jobs, positions, or cities every few years, which means that you need to constantly update the information. How do you do it? You have three real choices: Rolodex cards, a name and address book, or a computerized contact manager. (You also have a fourth choice, which is to not bother trying to keep track of any of these people. But if you go this route, your career will be brief.)

Let's look at the shortcomings of using either a Rolodex card file or a name and address book.

- **Rolodex cards quickly become unreadable.** How much information can you really store on a 2" x 4" or 3" x 5" card? If you're writing the names, addresses and phone numbers by hand, it won't take very long before the cards become beat up, dog eared, and dirty, especially if you're using them every day. And what happens to a card when you learn that something has changed in a person's life? You scratch out the old information and start scribbling the person's new company, address, and phone number on the card. To say the least, it soon becomes unreadable.

- **Name and address books quickly get beat up.** Keeping a name and address book can cause you even bigger problems. For starters, you must write each name, address, and phone number by hand, which can be an enormous waste of time. And after a couple of months of continuous use, a name and address book can get pretty beat up and messy because old numbers have been scratched out and replaced with the current numbers. It doesn't take very long before you've got a really big mess.

One day, my wife, Mitzi, and I were at a nearby park with our daughter DeLaine. While we were there, we watched a woman who was sitting on a park bench rewrite the list of names that were in her old address book into the new address book that she had just purchased. As Mitzi and I watched her, we said to each other, "Doesn't she have something more important to do?"

Put your names and addresses inside your computer

When you keep your list of names and addresses inside your computer, it's easy to keep everything up to date. Whenever a number changes, you just make the change to the person's record. And with just a few clicks of the mouse, you can add additional people to your contact manager or remove them from the program. After the names are inside your computer, you can use them for your mailing lists, phone lists, or even your Rolodex cards. Part IV tells you all about it.

Part IV

Working with ACT!

*A*re you tired of writing and rewriting information on the pages of your daily planner? Do you have a Rolodex file that's suffering from obesity? Is your name and address book falling apart? Have you collected hundreds, or thousands, of business cards that are gathering dust in the drawers of your desk? Would you like to make your life easier? Then put your daily planner, your Rolodex file, your name and address book, and all of those business cards inside your computer in an easy-to-use contact-management program.

With a contact manager, you can use the power of your computer to take control of all of your daily activities — your telephone calls, to-dos, meetings, and appointments. And you can use it to keep track of the names, addresses, and phone numbers of all the important people in your life. That's the main reason why you're using your computer in the first place: to help you get more work done in less time. A contact manager electronically links the basic components of your daily planner together. These components include your

- Calendar
- Appointment book
- To-do list
- Name and address book
- Notepad

There are many good contact-management programs available today, and I've tested a lot of them, but when all was said and done, the one that I liked the best was ACT!. I've found the ACT! contact-management program to be the best at keeping me on top of everything that's going on in both my business and personal life. And after you try ACT!, I'm sure you'll feel the same way.

On the following pages, I'm going to tell you how ACT! can help you to organize your day, help you stay on top of everything you've got to do, and make you more productive. If you're not currently using a contact-management program, it's my suggestion that you go out and purchase a copy of ACT! today. If you're using a different contact manager, I still think it would be worth your while to take a look at ACT!. It has some wonderful productivity-improving features.

ACT! is made by Symantec Corporation, 10201 Torre Avenue, Cupertino, CA 95014, 800-441-7234. (If you shop around, you should be able to purchase it for about $200 or less.) It's available in DOS, Windows, and Macintosh versions.

By the way, I would like to mention that I don't work for Symantec, and I don't own stock in the company. In fact, I have no relationship with the company at all. I'm just an everyday user who thinks ACT! is a very good productivity-improving tool. (I did, however, convince my editor at IDG Books to let me write the *ACT! For Dummies* book, which will be out in the summer of 1995.)

Why I Chose ACT! for My Contact Manager

In my most recent book, *Winning the Fight Between You and Your Desk,* I reviewed several dozen contact-management programs. I found the majority of them to be very powerful, and most were easy to use, but when I had finished writing my manuscript, I found myself faced with an unusual dilemma: Which contact-management program should I use for myself? There were so many good ones to choose from.

One of the programs I had previously evaluated was ACT!, which was, and still is, one of the most popular contact managers available. At the time I evaluated it, its cumulative sales were more than 500,000 copies (today its sales exceed 750,000). I decided to reinstall it on my computer and give it another try. After I played around with it for a few days, I discovered that it had the majority of the features that I would want in a computerized appointment book/calendar/to-do list program if I, as a time management expert, were to write such a program myself.

Today, I use ACT! all day long. It's the main reason I turn on my computer early in the morning, and ACT! is the last thing I turn off at the end of the day. ACT! does a wonderful job of keeping me on time and on top of everything that's going on in my life, both personally and professionally.

ACT! has a feature that will enable you to import all the names, addresses, and phone numbers that you've already entered into your current contact manager, personal information manager, computerized name and address book, or word processing merge file. This feature will save you the time and effort of reentering the same information a second time.

What ACT! Can Do for You

If you're like most people, I'm sure that you do many different things during the course of a normal business day:

- You schedule appointments with many different people.

- You have follow-up work to do.

- You have joint projects that you're working on with other people.

- You keep detailed notes of your telephone conversations and face-to-face meetings (or at least you're *supposed* to).

- You spend a lot of time on the phone.

- You send out letters, faxes, proposals, and other corre-spondence throughout the day.

With ACT!, you can manage all of these activities and tasks and more from inside your computer. You no longer need a Master List, a daily planner, and a calendar to stay organized. Any piece of information about a person, project, or task that you used to keep as a note in a file folder, as a scrap of paper on your desk, or as a mental note in your head can now be kept in one place — inside ACT!.

ACT! gives you a place to store the names, addresses, phone numbers, and lots of other information about your business and personal contacts, and ACT! integrates that information with your list of things to-do, your list of people to call, and your appointment calendar. After you start using ACT!, you'll find that fewer things slip through the cracks because everything's at your fingertips. The next two figures show you the front and back of an ACT! contact record.

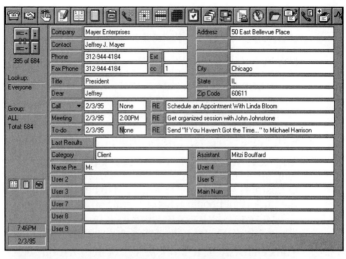

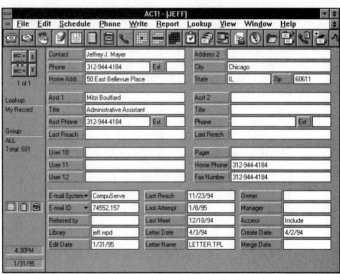

Improve your business relationships, lose weight, make friends, and influence people

Day in and day out, you're working and interacting with many people — customers, clients, and prospects, as well as your coworkers and colleagues — and you need to be able to stay on top of everything that's going on between you and them. With ACT!, you've got the tools you need to do a more thorough job of keeping track of all of the information that's associated with those projects, tasks, and all of your other daily activities.

And ACT! will also help you to develop and strengthen your long-term relationships — which is the key to being successful in business — because it's designed to help a person get to know the important people in his or her life on a more personal basis. ACT! gives you a place to store a lot of important information about a person and have it available at your fingertips.

You can use ACT! to store pieces of information such as the names of a person's spouse and children and the dates of their birthdays and anniversaries. And you can even use ACT! to take note of their hobbies, outside interests, favorite restaurants, and most recent vacations. You can store this information in addition to their many addresses and phone numbers (work, home, fax, car, and mobile) and the names and numbers of their assistants.

With ACT!, you have a place to routinely store little tidbits of miscellaneous information that you would otherwise forget.

How a beer can collection helped me sell some life insurance

When I started my business career as a Special Agent with Northwestern Mutual twenty-some years ago, I was taught to ask people a lot of questions about their personal, business, and financial situations. And during these interviews, I always made it a point to inquire about their outside interests and hobbies. One day, I was meeting with the treasurer of a large public company, and during the course of the conversation he mentioned that his son had a beer can collection, which I dutifully noted on my fact-finding form. When I came back a week later with my estate-planning presentation, he was so moved by the fact that I had remembered to make mention of the beer can collection that he bought a very large life insurance policy from me.

Turn your computer into an electronic Rolodex file

Whenever you meet someone new, you should always add that person's name to ACT!. When you're introduced to people at a business meeting, take their business cards and add their names to ACT!, and when you speak with new people on the phone, do the same thing: Add their names to your ACT! database.

You'll soon have the ability to keep in touch with hundreds, or thousands, of people easily and effortlessly. With ACT!'s very powerful Lookup feature, shown in the following figure, you can find any person's name and phone number in a fraction of a second.

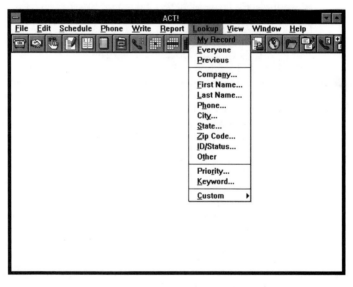

 I think the Lookup feature is one of the most important features in ACT! All you have to do is click Lookup with your mouse, select which criteria you want to look up (company, first name, last name, and so on) and then type the first few letters of the name, and the results of the search are displayed before you can blink your eyes. This sure beats trying to find someone's name in an ancient Rolodex file or an old, beat-up name and address book.

Go through those business cards that have been gathering dust in the lap drawer of your desk and put the information inside ACT!. Now you'll have a way to find these people when you need them.

 With CardScan, from Corex Technologies, you can scan your business cards directly into ACT!, thus eliminating the biggest hurdle we all have for getting this important information into your computers — typing it. (Cardscan, Corex Technologies Corp., 233 Harvard St., Brookline, MA 02146, 800-942-6739.)

 You can interface your ACT! database with Caller-ID with The Bridge to Caller-ID. After the first or second ring of your phone, The Bridge will identify who is calling, trigger your ACT! database, and display the person's record. For more information, contact The Bridge to Caller-ID, Postek Inc., 1857 Technology, Troy, MI 48083, 800-POSTEK-1.

Use the Lookup feature to help you plan your business trips

 Whenever you're scheduling a business trip, do a lookup for the names of all the people you know in the cities you're visiting. Then you can schedule some additional meetings or appointments while you're there. ACT! is also a great place to store the names of your favorite hotels and restaurants. With all of this information at your fingertips, what could be easier?

Don't rely on your memory, write it down

Have you ever had a conversation with a person and then wanted to write some brief notes to yourself regarding what was said? But you didn't bother because you didn't have a place to store the notes. And you knew that once you put them away, you would never find them again. With ACT!, you can overcome this dilemma because each person in ACT! has his or her own *notepad*. With the notepad, you can keep detailed notes of your telephone conversations and face-to-face meetings, thus eliminating the need to write notes to yourself on sticky notes or little pieces of paper that you'll never find again.

Each time you open the notepad, the current date is automatically entered in the left-hand margin. All you have to do is type the notes to yourself, close the notepad, and in just a few moments, you're going on to your next task. For ease of viewing, your previous entries are displayed in reverse chronological order.The notepad is shown in the following figure.

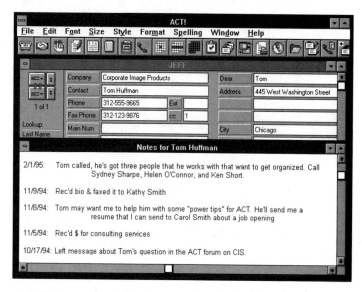

ACT! in action

As I was writing the section on ACT!'s notepad in WordPerfect for Windows, the phone rang. It was my friend John in Los Angeles, who was returning my call from earlier in the week. While John and I were exchanging greetings, I toggled over to ACT!, did a lookup of his last name, found his record, and opened the notepad. With the information therein, I was able to remind myself why I had called, check the date when we last spoke, and refresh my memory of the things we had spoken about previously. It took me no more than four seconds to do the whole process. While we were talking, he asked me to fax him a copy of a recent article about me that had appeared in the *New York Times,* so I clicked on ACT!'s To-Do icon, selected today's date, and typed in "Fax NYT article." When the conversation ended, I wrote a few brief notes to myself in the notepad and went back to work on this book.

Scheduling activities — calls, meetings, and to-dos — is a breeze

Do you have trouble remembering what you're supposed to do and when you're supposed to do it? Well, you're not alone. However, you can use ACT! to keep track of everything that you need to do. (Unfortunately, you've still got to do the work yourself.) ACT! makes scheduling activities — calls, meetings, or to-dos — easy because you hardly need to use the keyboard to enter any information. You can do almost all of it with just a few clicks of the mouse (see the next figure).

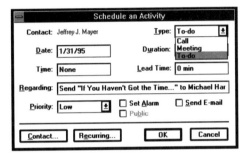

Whenever you need to schedule a task, the first thing you do is use the Lookup feature to find the person's record. (In ACT!, each task — a call, meeting, or to-do — is associated with a specific person; it's not itemized on a list.) Then you decide which type of activity you want to schedule and click on the appropriate icon.

After you click the icon, a pop-up monthly calendar appears where you select a date. A mini-day calendar pops up where you can select the activity's starting time and duration. Then you can enter a brief description for this activity from the keyboard in the Regarding field or select an item — send proposal, send quote, send follow-up letter, confirm meeting, schedule lunch, and so on — from the pop-up box, which contains frequently used phrases or terms that describe the specific nature of your daily activities. You can assign priority levels to each activity, and if you want to be reminded of an activity, you can set the alarm.

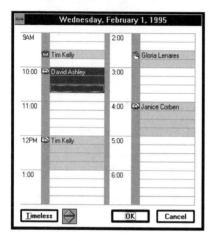

An alarming ACT!

I once called someone who said to me, "I can't talk to you right now. Would you call me back in 20 minutes?" In the past, I would have put this person's file aside and promptly forgotten about him. But on this afternoon, I came up with what I thought was a *brilliant* idea: Why not use ACT!'s alarm to remind me of the call? So I clicked on the Call icon and set the alarm; 20 minutes later, I made the call.

Picture your appointments

After you've scheduled meetings and appointments, ACT! gives you several different ways to see with whom you're meeting and when you're meeting them. With a click of the mouse, you can see your appointment calendar in a daily, weekly, or monthly format so that you can see a "picture" of what your future time commitments look like. And when you're looking at your calendar, you can schedule new appointments, modify existing appointments, or clear appointments, all with the click of the mouse. The next three figures show the daily, monthly, and weekly calendars, respectively.

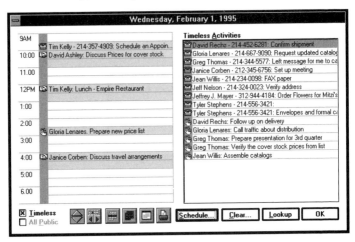

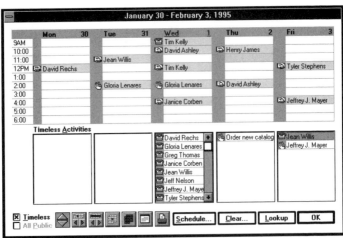

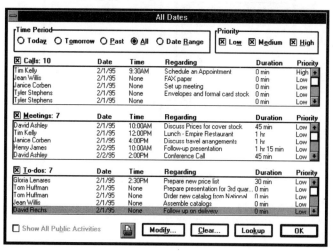

Besides viewing your activities in a calendar format, you also have the ability to view all of your tasks — calls, meetings, and to-dos — on a single list, which is conveniently called the Task List. (Creative people, those software designers.) Just press a button or click an icon with your mouse, and your list of current tasks appears. And with another click of your mouse, you can see a list of all your past, present, or future calls, meetings, or to-dos. The following figure shows the ACT! Task List.

The ACT! Automatic Information Entry System

Most people hate typing. And one of the most time-consuming and time-wasting parts of using a database is entering repetitive information. It becomes really boring typing the same city, state, and ZIP code, such as "CHICAGO, IL 60611" over and over again. ACT! has a simple way of dealing with that problem. It uses pop-up dialog boxes.

A *pop-up* dialog box is a box that pops up when the cursor is moved onto a specific field. The box can be set up so that it pops up automatically, or on request (by pressing F2 or double-clicking with the mouse). In the pop-up dialog box, you then select an item from a list, and that item is automatically inserted into the field. Any field in ACT! can be designated a pop-up, or an automatic pop-up field. To enter the information in the City field, for example, you just use your cursor to select the city you want, or you can just type a letter: Type **C** for Chicago, **N** for New York, **L** for Los Angeles, and so on. Then press Enter, and the city's name is automatically inserted.

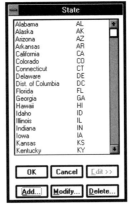

Every field in ACT! can have a pop-up dialog box that can be customized to display the specific words or phrases that you use to describe your daily business activities.

Store and dial phone numbers in Act!

ACT! is designed to store all of a person's telephone numbers. These could include the person's main office number, a phone number at a second or third location, as well as a home number, a beeper number, an e-mail address, and a fax number. ACT! can also store the secretary or assistant's name and phone numbers.

When you want to place a call, all you have to do is click on the Phone icon, and a list of all of the person's phone numbers is displayed in a pop-up dialog box.

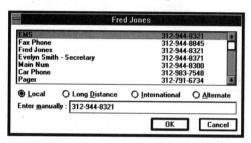

If your computer and your telephone share the same line, you can use the computer to dial the phone, and after the call goes through, all you have to do is pick up the receiver and begin your conversation. If your computer doesn't have a modem or it's not connected to your voice telephone line, you click on the phone list, select the number you want to call, and dial it manually. This method sure beats trying to find a number in an old, beat-up Rolodex file.

Unlimited Systems makes a little black box, called Konnex, that enables you to connect your computer's fax modem to a digital, PBX, or multiline phone system so that you can take advantage of ACT!'s autodialing capability. (Konnex, Unlimited Systems, 8586 Miramar Place, San Diego, CA 92121, 800-275-6354.)

Categories anyone?

Categorizing people makes it easy to find selected groups of people. One of the features that makes ACT! so powerful is its capability to group people in different categories based on their business, profession, or any other criteria you might select. You can then do a lookup of this group, and in a few moments, you have a complete listing of everyone in that particular group. The Category pop-up dialog box it makes it very easy to enter this information.

I left my Rolodex in San Francisco

I do all of my own publicity and have set up categories for newspaper, magazine, radio, television, and so on. To date, I've stored the names of more than a thousand newspaper, magazine, radio, television, and other media people in my database. With the Lookup feature, I can do some amazing things with all this information. For example, in just a few seconds, I can create a list of the people who work for a radio station in Dallas and write for a newspaper in San Francisco. How long would it take you to gather such information with your Rolodex file? ACT! really puts the power of your computer at your fingertips.

Let ACT! write your letters

ACT! has a built-in word processor that makes it easy for you to write letters, memos, e-mails, and faxes. Just select the person to whom you want to send a letter and then click the Letter icon. The basic format of the letter will be created in an instant. This format includes the date, the person's name and address, salutation, and your closing. All you have to do is write the text. You can then print the letter, fax the letter (ACT! works with WinFax Pro), or send it as electronic mail.

If you have some form letters that you send out regularly, you can use ACT!'s mail-merge feature to merge the form letter template with a single person or a group of people. ACT! comes with predesigned letter templates that can be easily modified so that you can create your own customized letters, memos, and faxes. You also can print the information you've stored in ACT! as a telephone directory, mailing labels, envelopes, or Rolodex cards.

Does your boss want to know what you've been doing?

One of the biggest timesaving features of ACT! is its capability to take any of the different pieces of information that you have about each person in your database and use that information to create reports. You can generate reports of all your daily activities (your calls, meetings, and to-dos) and include any notes you may have taken about the various people in your file. You can display a history of what you've done with those people in the past and create a detailed list of the calls, meetings, and to-dos that you have scheduled with them in the future. These reports can be created for a single individual or a group of people.

If ACT!'s report-generating capabilities aren't powerful enough for you, you may want to give Crystal Reports a try. With Crystal Reports, you can create personalized management reports, lead lists, forecast reports, statistical summaries, mailing labels, and much more. (Crystal Reports, Crystal Services, 1050 West Pender Street, Suite 2200, Vancouver, B.C., Canada V6E 3S7, 800-877-2340 (US).)

Use ACT!; save money

Several years ago, I was having some difficulty getting reimbursed for the telephone expenses I incurred as part of the ongoing publicity for one of my books. One day, I got a letter from my publisher's publicity department stating that they would be happy to reimburse me for those expenses, but I would have to provide them with the names of everyone I spoke with, the dates we spoke, and the current status of the publicity that was being generated. They thought they were being cute because nobody could possibly create such a list without spending hours and hours of time trying to put it together.

But they didn't know that I was using ACT!. I just printed a contact report for my entire "media" database — which had more than a thousand people in it — and put the 400-page report in the mail. Two weeks later, I received my check for almost 2,000 dollars.

Share your ACT!

One of the extremely powerful features of ACT! is that it is network compatible. This feature enables you to share a common database and have access to another person's database.

You can take it with you

If you love your daily planner and can't live without it, you can print information from any part of ACT! (on a variety of paper sizes), insert the pages into your favorite daily planner, and take it with you as you walk out the door. This feature enables you to have the best of both worlds: a computer program that keeps you on top of everything that's going on in your life and a paper-based program that you can take with you when you're away from your office.

Part V

Working in Your Home Office

*A*lmost all of us do some kind of work out of our homes. Some of us have set up our own businesses; others work out of their homes while continuing to work for large companies; and still others may run a part-time or second business from home while working a full-time job elsewhere. And finally, everybody else has a home office in which they pay their bills, write their letters, and have a place to store their computer.

You need to be organized

If you're going to work out of your home, you've got to be organized. And that's the subject that I address in the Part I of this book. If you haven't read Part I, I would suggest that you go back and do so now. If you would like more detailed information about how to get organized, you should read my first best-seller, *If You Haven't Got the Time to Do It Right, When Will You Find the Time to Do It Over?*

You need a good follow-up system

You also need a good follow-up system so that you can stay on top of all of your unfinished work, tasks, and projects. If you don't have a good follow-up system, important things often slip through the cracks, leaving you with a time-consuming problem that could easily have been avoided. The subject of how to set up a good follow-up system is discussed in Part II of this book, in which I discuss how you can master your day with your Master List.

You need to use ACT!

The process of staying organized has evolved from keeping a Master List of all your things to do on a big piece of paper to maintaining a list of all of your unfinished tasks — your calls, meetings, and to-dos — inside your computer. And that's what ACT! does. It gives you the ability to automate the whole process of staying on top of your unfinished work and eliminates the need to keep track of things with a pencil and a piece of paper. For a complete description of how ACT! can help you become more productive, efficient, and effective, you should read Part IV, if you haven't done so already. (I use ACT! 10 to 12 hours per day and think the program is so important that I convinced the people at IDG Books to let me write *ACT! For Dummies,* which will be published in the summer of 1995.)

Where Should I Put My Home Office?

Depending upon your usage requirements and your available space, you can put a home office almost anywhere. You can work out of the kitchen, dining room, bedroom, a second or unused bedroom, the attic, or the basement. But wherever you put your home office, you must think of it as a *real* office. If possible, you should stay away from high-traffic, high-noise, areas. And the people you live with — your family, significant other, or roommate — should accept the fact that when you're in your office, you're working. Let them know that when you're in your office, you need privacy and shouldn't be disturbed.

Setting up your home office

After you've decided where your office will be located, you've got to set it up. That means you need a desk or table, chair, telephone, fax machine, filing space, a computer, and a lot of other things. The manner in which you set up your home office depends upon what type of work you'll be doing and how many hours a day you'll be doing it. So here are some questions to ask yourself:

- Will you be sitting at your computer for a good portion of the day?

- Will you be writing things by hand, as opposed to typing them into the computer?

- How many hours per day will you be on the telephone?

- Will you be meeting with customers or clients in your home office?

Selecting a desk

Because you're going to have a home office, you need to have a desk.

When you select a desk, you should first determine how large you want it to be. And then you should address the question of drawer space.

You can have a desk with several small drawers, a lap drawer, a file drawer, or a combination thereof. You may even decide that you would just like to have a flat work surface without any drawers and use something else to hold your files, papers, and other miscellaneous things. (Steelcase Inc., Grand Rapids, MI 49501, the world's largest manufacturer and designer of office systems, offers a complete line of home office desks and furnishings. To locate your nearest Steelcase dealer, call 800-333-9939.)

Selecting a chair

After you've selected your work surface, you've got to find the right chair because you'll be sitting in it every day for hours at a time. Sitting for long periods of time in an uncomfortable chair, like sleeping on an uncomfortable mattress, can result in health problems, especially backaches. Backaches and other illnesses translate into lost productivity. In fact, if you're suffering from backaches and/or your legs are going to sleep, you may be the victim of a poorly designed chair.

Sit in a chair that fits your body

A well-designed chair is one that adjusts to the shape of your body and allows you to find comfortable positions while you're working. Once it is properly adjusted, it not only supports your back, but it also reduces the strain on your shoulders, neck, arms, and hands. These are some of the features you should look for in a chair:

- The seat height should be easily adjustable. When sitting at your computer, your elbows should be at the same height as the keyboard. If the keyboard is sitting on the desktop, the height of your seat will probably need to be raised to a height that is higher than you're normally accustomed to. As a result, your feet will no longer be resting comfortably on the floor. To compensate, you'll need a footrest to support your feet. If the keyboard height is adjustable, then you can lower the height of your seat so that your feet will comfortably reach the floor.

- The back rest should be adjustable up and down and should fit the curve of your lower back. You want your back to be fully supported so that you can sit up straight, with your head positioned directly over your shoulders. Your arms should be resting comfortably at your sides. If you need additional back support, use cushions or foam padding.

- The seat cushion should have a slight forward slope and shouldn't dig into the back of your legs. This takes the pressure off the spine and transfers it to the thighs and feet.

- The arms should be adjustable so that you can change the height and angle of each arm, allowing the chair to conform to the shape of your body.

- The chair should swivel left and right, tilt forward and backward, and roll on casters. These features give you more mobility and ease of motion, making that task of trying to reach something that is slightly out of reach much easier.

The most comfortable office chair I ever sat in

Every feature that I have just described has been incorporated into the Criterion chair from Steelcase. It is by far the most comfortable office chair I have ever used.

- Fitting the chair to both the job and the body of the person who is using it can be quite a challenge. Steelcase not only includes every possible adjustment in its Criterion chair, but it has made the adjustments very easy to use.

- The feature that I like the most is the individually adjustable arm rests that are designed to support the hands and forearms. When you're typing, your hands aren't resting on the keyboard; they're floating over the keyboard.

- I can honestly say that my Criterion chair has gotten a lot of use. I've been sitting in it for six, eight, or ten hours per day for almost two years, and I can assure you that it would have been impossible for me to spend so many hours at the computer in a chair that wasn't as well designed as the Criterion. Criterion chairs come with either a high- or a mid-back. The arm rests are optional. For a catalog and a current price list, call 800-333-9939.

Creating a Healthy Work Environment

We all come in different shapes and sizes — some of us are tall; others are short; one person may have large hands; another person's hands may be petite. Because of this, you need to be able to adjust your work area to fit your own physical needs. To create a working environment that is right for you, you must take a number of different factors into consideration: the height of your desk, chair, and keyboard; the position of your monitor; and the intensity of the interior lighting under which you're working. If your office equipment forces you to sit in an unnatural position — especially if your wrists are cocked — your risk of injury is greatly increased.

Up until now, you've probably never given any thought regarding how you should position yourself at the keyboard. Most people position the height of their chair so that their feet rest comfortably on the floor, without any regard to the position of their hands in relation to the keyboard. A better way is to make sure your hands are properly positioned at the keyboard — then make any other necessary adjustments.

Position your hands properly on the keyboard

When sitting at the keyboard, you want to type with a flat wrist, positioned at or just below elbow level, so that your forearms are at a 90-degree angle to your upper arms. Your arms should rest comfortably at your sides; your wrists should be relaxed; and your fingers should be gently curved. Typing with a cocked wrist, either upward or downward, places extra stress on the tendons and nerves as they pass through the wrist. Sitting in a chair that is either too high or too low in relation to their keyboards often causes people to type with cocked wrists.

If the height of the keyboard is adjustable, it's easy to achieve this 90-degree position. If the keyboard is sitting on a desk or table whose height cannot be changed, you can compensate for this by raising your chair to the proper height and using a footrest to support your feet.

Here are some keyboard tips:

- If the keyboard is too large for your hands or fingers, try to reach the outlying keys by lifting your hand and arm from the shoulder rather than twisting your wrists or straining to reach those keys with your fingers.

- When typing, avoid resting your wrists on the edge of the work surface. Doing so can put additional pressure on those same tendons and nerves that you're trying to treat so gingerly.

- To reduce the strain on your wrists, muscles, and tendons, consider using a padded wrist or palm rest that you can place in front of the keyboard. A wrist rest can be especially helpful during brief typing breaks.

- When typing, keep your hands relaxed, type gently, and don't pound the keys.

If your hands hurt, try a different keyboard

I spend a lot of time at my computer keyboard, and after a while my hands, fingers, and forearms begin to ache. Somehow I don't think that the human body was designed to spend hours on end typing away. So after a few visits to my favorite massage therapist, I decided to try one of those fancy ergonomic keyboards. A few days later, my Kinesis Ergonomic Keyboard arrived in the mail, and after using it for a few days, my hands stopped hurting. I've now written two books with it, and I just love it.

Kinesis's designers have given a lot of thought and consideration as to how the human hand and body relate to the keyboard, and they've done some neat things in their design of the keyboard. (The keyboard looks more like the control panel from the Starship Enterprise than a computer keyboard.)

- The keyboard is divided into two concave wells that are placed six inches apart. This feature separates the user's hands, allowing the elbows and arms to rest at shoulder width.

- The keys are positioned in a slight arc, instead of in a straight line, which takes into consideration that your fingers are of different lengths — thus conforming the keyboard to the shape of the hand.

- They repositioned the keys that were formerly pressed with the little finger — the Backspace, Delete, Ctrl, Alt, Home, End, Page Up, Page Down, Enter and Space keys — and grouped them together in two sets of thumb pads.

- They added a foot pedal that can be used in place of the Shift key and have included a little bit of memory into the keyboard so that you can record keyboard macros and save yourself the time and effort of retyping the same words or program commands over and over and over.

If you've been experiencing finger, hand, or arm discomfort, the Kinesis Ergonomic Keyboard is certainly worth trying. **Kinesis Ergonomic Keyboard.** Kinesis Corporation, 915 118th Avenue Southeast, Bellevue, WA 98005, 800-454-6374.

Position your monitor so that you don't have to lean forward

After you've discovered the proper position for your body in relation to the keyboard, you need to address the position of your monitor. Here are some tips:

- The top of the monitor should be positioned so that it's even with or slightly below your forehead. You should be able to look straight at the screen without being forced to tilt your head forward and downward.

- A monitor support arm can be used to raise your monitor to the desired height. These arms allow the monitor to "float" above the desktop and offer tremendous flexibility because you can position them at any height and distance from your eyes that you want. (I've raised my monitor almost six inches by placing several books under it.)

- Position your monitor in such a way as to minimize on-screen glare. (If it's impossible to find such a position, place an anti-glare screen on the monitor or attach a visor-like hood over the top.)

- To make the task of typing easier and at the same time reduce the strain on your neck, attach a copy holder to the side of your monitor. The copy holder holds the papers right next to the screen, minimizing eye and neck movement.

A footrest improves your circulation

A footrest is an important — and often overlooked — piece of office furniture. It can reduce the pressure on the back of your thighs, minimize lower back strain by raising your feet, and improve the circulation of blood throughout your body. Most importantly, it compensates for the lack of flexibility between your chair and your desk. By supporting your legs and feet, it allows you to sit higher than would normally be comfortable.

Filing and Storage Space

After you've made the decision about the type of desk and chair you want, you next have to give consideration to how you want to store your papers, documents, and office supplies. If you don't want to purchase a traditional multidrawer filing cabinet, you have some alternatives. For example, you could purchase a small filing cabinet — with one file drawer and one small drawer — that rolls on a caster and is small enough to fit under a table. Or maybe you would like to put all of your files and papers in a dresser so the room doesn't look so much like an office.

Use expandable filing pockets

In Part I, I talk about how you can use expandable file pockets to make your filing system work better. You can use the expandable file pockets in other ways in addition to putting them inside filing cabinets. For example, you can put your papers inside an expandable file pocket and then put it on a shelf inside one of your closets. With a black marker, you can write a name or title that describes the contents of the expandable file pocket on the side of the file pocket that faces out.

 To conserve space and save yourself the cost of purchasing a filing cabinet, install adjustable shelves in a closet and put your expandable file pockets on the shelves. (That's what I've done.)

Buy a dresser

As an alternative to purchasing a filing cabinet, you can also use a dresser as a place to store all of your files, papers, and all of the other things you need to run your business from your home. You can then use the top of the dresser as a place to put your printer and fax machine.

Install shelves on your walls

One of the best ways to get papers, files, books, software manuals, and lots of other miscellaneous things off your desk, is to hang shelves on the wall and put all of this *stuff* on the shelves.

Don't leave everything in piles

Whatever you end up doing, don't leave everything in piles; it's just impossible to get your work done, do it well, and get it done on time. If you still have piles all over the place, it's time to read (or reread) Part I of this book.

Home Office Lighting

Many people don't give enough consideration to the lighting in their home office. You can simply be much more productive when you've got the right type of light to perform a specific task. You should design your office with the knowledge that the lighting you need to read a letter, for example, is different than the lighting you need to work at your computer.

Your goal is to create a work environment where the light's bright enough for you to easily read your papers and documents, while at the same time providing enough indirect light so that you can work at your computer without seeing glare or reflections on your screen.

To control the amount of daylight that's coming into your home office, install adjustable blinds. The direct sunlight can be blocked, filtered, or redirected by adjusting the angle of the blades.

If you're getting glare off your computer's monitor, it's time to buy a new one. All new monitors have antiglare glass.

Setting Up Your Telephone System

If you're going to be running a business out of your home, you've got to treat it like a business, and that means you need to have a proper telephone system. Whatever your needs, you have a lot of options. So here are some thoughts about phone systems.

You need at least two lines

To run a business properly, you need to have at least two telephone lines; otherwise, your customers and clients will all too frequently receive busy signals.

My wife, Mitzi, and I both run our respective businesses out of our home. (She's an interior designer, and I'm a time management consultant and author.) When we installed our phone system, we put in two lines with call-waiting on the second line. Here's how it works: If someone calls on line one and it's in use, the call is automatically transferred to line two. If both lines are busy, the call-waiting feature is activated on the second line. This system has worked for us for almost ten years now. (Someday we may get a third line, but so far it hasn't been necessary.)

Do you need a line for your fax machine?

Fax machines have become a major part of all of our business lives. It's almost impossible to imagine conducting business without one today. If you send and receive a lot of faxes it may be worth the expense of installing a dedicated line solely for your fax machine. You do, however, have some other choices. Here are a few of them.

Share your fax and voice lines

Your local telephone company may have a service that uses a single line that can distinguish between a voice call and a fax call. When you get a fax, the call is routed to your fax machine, and when you get a voice call, your telephone rings.

Buy a switching box

You can purchase a small switching box that automatically routes your calls. If you receive a fax, the call goes to the fax machine; otherwise, your telephone rings. One of the neat features of the switching box is that you can answer the phone from anywhere in the house; by pressing 0, you can send the call to the answering machine; and by pressing another number, 22 for example, you can send the call to your fax machine.

Many of the new fax machines already have switching boxes installed.

To solve the problem of how to get our single-line answering machine and single-line fax machine to answer the call when either of our two telephone lines begins to ring, we bought a routing box at Radio Shack for about $15. Whenever the phone rings, it doesn't matter if it's on line one or line two, the routing box sends the call to the switching box, which then sends the call to the answering machine if it's a voice call or the fax machine if it's a fax. The routing box saved us the expense of purchasing a two-line answering machine and a two-line fax machine (which I don't think exists).

Do you need a line for your computer?

If you spend a lot of time on-line, you may want to consider installing a separate line for your computer. When your computer and telephone share the same line, you can use the computer to dial the phone for you. The autodialing feature is one of the very powerful features of ACT! and many other contact managers.

You do need a telephone!

We all seem to take the telephone for granted. We're accustomed to having fancy phone systems at our offices but don't think about giving ourselves the same conveniences in our home offices. You should consider having some of the following features on your phone:

- Buttons for two or more lines
- Conference calling
- Speed dialing
- Speaker phone

Panasonic makes a complete line of telephones for the home office. In addition to one-, two-, and three-line phones, Panasonic makes telephones that have built-in paging and intercom systems, in addition to telephones that are Caller I.D. compatible. **Panasonic.** Panasonic Company , One Panasonic Way, Secaucus, NJ 07094. For the name of your nearest Panasonic dealer, call 201-348-9090.

Use a telephone headset

Does your neck ever get stiff from cradling the telephone handset between your ear, chin, and shoulder? Do you find it difficult to take notes while you're on the phone — because you just can't find an easy way to hold the phone to your left ear, use your left elbow to keep the pad of paper from moving, write with your right hand, and remain comfortable all at the same time?

If you answered "Yes" to either of these questions, you should be using a telephone headset instead of the traditional handset. In fact, if you spend any time at all on the phone, you should be using a telephone headset. I've been using one for years and have found that it's not only comfortable, but it has greatly improved my productivity and efficiency as well.

Today's headsets are so light and comfortable that once you put one on, you'll quickly forget that you're even wearing it. And when you're on the phone, you'll have the use of both of your hands so that you can concentrate on the conversation instead of the pain in your neck or the tenderness in your ear.

Plantronics makes a full line of headsets for both corporate users and people that run businesses out of their homes. **Plantronics.** 345 Encinal Street, Santa Cruz, CA 95060. For a catalog and a current price list, call 800-426-5858.

Who's going to answer your phone?

If you're going to be running a business out of your home, someone's got to answer your phone when you're not there. Depending upon your needs and your budget, you have a number of choices.

Get an answering machine

The easiest thing you can do is purchase an answering machine. Today you have lots of choices. You can purchase just a simple, no frills machine, a machine that can answer two or three lines, or something in between.

Panasonic's newest answering machines feature digital sound for both the incoming and outgoing messages. Because the answering machine is digital, you have the capability of creating individual mailboxes so that you can organize your messages. And with digital recording, the sound is crystal clear. **Panasonic.** Panasonic Company, One Panasonic Way, Secaucus, NJ 07094. For the name of your nearest Panasonic dealer, call 201-348-9090.

Hire an answering service

If you want a *real* person to answer your phone instead of a machine with a recorded message, you should look into hiring an answering service.

Get a voice mail system

Your local telephone company may offer a full-service voice mail system, with which you can record your own messages and call at any time of the day or night to hear the messages that you've received. These messages can be saved or archived for future reference.

Get More out of Your Present Computer

If you're going to run a business out of your home, you *must* have a computer. In this section I give you some tips on how you can get more out of your present computer.

Every morning, I look at the newspaper and see that the prices for new computers keep on dropping. When I bought my first word processor — a dedicated word processor, not a computer — it cost me almost $2000, plus another $500 for a sheet feeder. (Yes, that's right.) And that was only in 1988. (I bought my first computer in 1990). Today, you can buy a Pentium computer with a monitor and a printer for $2500.

Now don't get nervous. I'm not writing this section because I think you should go out and purchase a new computer this very minute. (In the following section I'll tell you what bells and whistles I think you should have on your next computer.) I'm writing this section of the book because there are a lot of things you can do with your present machine to improve its performance without replacing it. At some point, you *will* have to replace it, but you may be able to put off the new purchase for a year; by then computers will be even cheaper. (If you're wondering why I'm including information on computers in a time management book, the answer is easy: When you're sitting at your computer and nothing's happening, you're wasting time. And since time is money, you should get the most out of your computer.)

Some of the things I mention in the next few pages are a bit technical. If you're not familiar with the insides and inner workings of a computer, don't try to do any of these things yourself. Just invite your favorite computer guru over for dinner, and then casually ask him or her to help you with a *little* project.

If you're still using a 286 or 386, it's time to replace it!

OK, I lied. You should get nervous. If you're still using an old 286, or a not-quite-so-old 386 computer, you don't have to read any further. Your machine is too old to be saved. It just doesn't have the horsepower to take you through the 90s. It's like driving a 1969 Volkswagen, or maybe a 1974 Volkswagen. It may take you where you want to go, but then again, it may not make it. I suggest you immediately turn to the section titled "Bells and Whistles for Your Next Computer."

Get a memory manager

This suggestion is easy: You can do it on almost any PC, and you don't have to take the machine apart. You just install some new software. No matter how much RAM — 4MB, 8MB, 16MB — you have in your computer, a memory manager will improve its performance. (RAM is the stuff that lets you run your word processor, spreadsheet programs, and everything else.) It's only the first 1024K of memory, also called the first megabyte, that's used to run your computer. Of this first megabyte of memory, conventional memory takes up the first 640K, and high memory takes up the balance, 384K.

Conventional memory is important because all your important software — your word processor, spreadsheet, solitaire, minesweeper, and so on — run in conventional memory. When you have more conventional memory available, your programs run better.

Without going into all the gory details, a memory manager takes all the miscellaneous things that your computer had been placing in conventional memory, things that had been using up a good chunk of that 640K, and puts them in the high memory. Therefore, you have more memory for your programs. Quarterdeck Office System's QEMM (QEMM is an acronym for Quarterdeck Expanded Memory Manager) makes a very powerful memory manager. When I first installed QEMM several years ago, I was able to increase my available conventional memory from 543K to 619K, an increase of 13 percent. I recently installed Quarterdeck's most recent version and increased my available conventional memory to 634K. Now I'm able to allocate more than 99 percent of my available memory for my software. **QEMM.** Quarterdeck Office Systems, 150 Pico Blvd., Santa Monica, CA 90405, 800-354-3222.

Double the capacity of your hard drive

There was a time when a 40MB hard drive was sufficient to hold all of your programs. Today, *suites* — packages of programs that often include a word processor, spreadsheet, database, and graphics program — take more than 40MB all by themselves. And with software developers continuing to add more bells and whistles to their programs with each product upgrade, it's easy to run out of disk storage space.

If you're running out of storage space on your hard drive, you do have an alternative if you're not ready to replace your hard drive. You can install a data-compression program that will effectively double the capacity of your hard drive.

A data-compression program does something really neat: It's able to shrink the size of your files. As a general rule, you can compress word processing files to about half their original size. Database and spreadsheet files compress even more. Program files don't compress very much.

After you've compressed your disk drive, you still use your computer just as you did before. When you open a file, the data is decompressed and expands back to its original size for use within your program. When you save the file, it's automatically recompressed to save space. It all happens so quickly that you aren't aware that anything's happening. The only thing you do notice is that you can store twice as much data on your hard drive. Stacker is the leading disk compression program. **Stacker.** Stacker Electronics, 5993 Avenida Encinas, Carlsbad, CA 92008, 800-522-7822.

If you still need more disk space, get a new hard drive

A data-compression program is a great way to get more out of your current hard drive, but it's only going to buy you some time. Sooner or later, you're going to run out of hard disk space. And when that happens, you have two choices: You can add a second disk drive to your computer, if you don't want to replace your original disk drive, or you can go out and replace the old hard drive with one of those new, huge 500MB or 1000MB (gigabyte) disk drives.

There is an important reason why it's in your best interest to replace your old disk drive with a new one, in addition to the fact that the new drives are so much bigger. The new drives read the data on the hard drive much more quickly than the older drives, so your whole system runs faster.

Seagate Technology makes a complete line of hard disk drives. Their newest drive, the Decathlon 850 (ST5850A), has a capacity of 850MB. It uses Seagate's fast ATA technology and can transfer data from the hard drive to the computer's central processing unit (CPU) at speeds of up to 16 MB/second.

Installing the Seagate drive in my computer was rather easy. The instructions that came with the hard drive were very thorough and comprehensive. (Before I do anything with my computer, I *always* call tech support just to see whether there's anything additional I should know. This has helped me stay out of trouble.) When I called the tech support line at Seagate, the person who answered the phone was not only helpful, but she actually walked me through the entire installation process. But once again, if you've never done this kind of thing before, ask your favorite computer guru to come over to help you with a *little* project.

With the new Seagate hard drive, my various programs — WordPerfect, ACT!, and everything else I use on my computer — run faster because the access time — the time it takes to read and write information from the hard drive to the computer's memory — is much faster. (In fact, the Decathlon 850 transfers data so fast that my computer can't keep up with it. I guess it's time to get a Pentium. But that's another story.) The faster your computer runs, the more productive you are. **Seagate Technology.** 920 Disk Drive, Scotts Valley, CA 95066. To find your nearest Seagate dealer, call 800-468-3472.

Add a cache controller card

You've probably never heard of a cache controller card, also known as a disk accelerator, but even though you don't know what they do, they can do a lot to make your computer run faster. A cache controller card handles the flow of data from your hard drive to your computer's central processing unit (CPU). On some systems, it's able to reduce the read and write access time from the hard drive to the CPU from 9-12 ms (milliseconds, or thousandths of a second) to 0.1 ms.

After I took the top off my computer, I just pulled out the old controller card, inserted the new one, and reattached the cable that runs from the card to the hard drive. To say it was easy is an understatement. When I turned my computer back on, I could see that everything was running faster. Promise Technologies makes a full line of cache controller cards. **Promise Technologies.** 1460 Koll Circle, San Jose, CA 95112. For a products catalog or for the number of the nearest computer store that carries Promise Technologies' cache controller cards, call 800-888-0245.

Get a new video card

If you think that all of your programs are running just a bit too slowly, or if you've just gotten into multimedia and CD-ROMs, and everything appears on your screen in slow motion, it may not be your computer that's slowing you down. It may be your video card. Even though you just purchased a super-fast computer, the computer manufacturer may have installed last year's video card, one with only 1MB of memory, in order to keep the price down.

Today's video cards can really make your computer fly. I replaced my old video card with a Diamond Stealth 64 with 4MB of memory. When I turned my computer on, I couldn't believe how much faster it ran. I didn't notice too much of a difference when I was working in WordPerfect because the screen doesn't redraw itself that frequently. But when I started using my graphics programs, the images on the screen redrew themselves in just a fraction of a second, with 16 million colors.

I would have to estimate that my graphics programs are now running five to ten times faster than they were before. It's also done the same thing to my CD-ROMs. And, if you're one of those people who likes to play games on your computer, a faster video card will make a world of difference. Diamond Computer Systems makes a full line of video cards. **Diamond Computer Systems.** Diamond Computer Systems, 2880 Junction Avenue, San Jose, CA 95134-1922, 800-468-5846.

Improve your vision with a new monitor

If you're using an old monitor or your current monitor is smaller than 15 inches, it may be time to give the old one away and buy a new one. A new monitor can make a world of difference to your daily productivity. If you have to over-concentrate to read the words on your monitor because of either low resolution or small screen size, the muscles in your neck and shoulders become tense — and you get tired. With a new 15-, 17-, or 21-inch monitor, there will be such a substantial increase in your productivity that it will pay for itself in a matter of weeks.

When I recently upgraded my computer, I replaced my old monitor with a Nanao 15-inch color monitor. I didn't know what I had been missing until I plugged it into my computer and turned it on. The first things I noticed were the increases in size, clarity, and brightness. And with the flat, nonglare screen, I no longer needed a visor to keep the glare from the lights in my office off my monitor. Furthermore, Nanao's WideView screen provides an edge-to-edge viewing area.

I also didn't realize until after I changed monitors how much I was straining to read the text on my screen because of the small screen size and the low resolution. Now I know how people feel when they come back from the eye doctor with a new set of eyeglasses. I can see clearly again. In fact, I no longer need to have the monitor so close to me. **Nanao USA Corporation.** 23535 Telo Avenue, Torrance, CA 90505. Nanao makes a complete line of high- and ultra-high-resolution color monitors from 15 inches to 21 inches. For a catalog and a current price list, call 800-800-5202.

Add more memory

Earlier in this part, I mention the importance of using a memory manager to make your computer run more efficiently. In the old days, before Windows, you could only run one program at a time, so the amount of memory wasn't a big concern. Today, it's a big deal! One of the beautiful things about Windows is that you can run one, two, three, four, or more programs simultaneously if you have enough memory. And the more memory you have, the faster these programs will run.

If your computer has only 4MB of memory, it's time to call your computer guru friend and invite him or her over for dinner. After dessert, you can ask your "guest" to put some more memory into your computer. It's not difficult to do, if you know what you're doing.

Some of the newer programs, like WordPerfect 6.1, need at least 8MB of memory to run properly. (I've heard through the grapevine that you won't even be able to run Windows 95, Microsoft's next version of Windows, with less than 8MB of memory.)

I recently increased my computer's memory from 8MB to 16MB, and I can see a huge improvement in my computer's performance. My computer programs run faster, and I can have more of them open at the same time. Kingston Technology Corporation makes a complete line of memory upgrade modules that can increase your computer's memory to 8MB, 16MB, 32MB, 64MB, and beyond. **Kingston Technology Corporation.** 17600 Newhope Street, Fountain Valley, CA 92708, 800-835-6575.

Upgrade your 486 computer to a Pentium

If you already own a 486 computer, but it's a year or two old, you can now upgrade your computer to a Pentium by using one of Intel's new Pentium OverDrive processors. With more processing power, you'll be able to crunch the numbers on your spreadsheets much more quickly; your multimedia programs will run faster; and you'll have more power to play your games.

To install an OverDrive processor, all you've got to do is remove the old computer chip from your computer and insert the new one in its place. (But once again, if you don't know the ins and outs of computers, invite your computer guru friend over for dinner.) **Intel OverDrive Processor.** Intel Corporation, 2200 Mission College Blvd., Santa Clara, CA 95051, 800-538-3373.

Protect your computer from viruses

Do you do any of the following:

- Do you ever download programs from private bulletin board services (BBSs)?

- Do you ever copy files from other systems by using floppy disks?

- Are you hooked up to a local-area network (LAN)?

If you answered "Yes" to any of these questions, your computer could easily become infected with a computer virus.

What is a computer virus? It's an infectious computer program that makes your computer do weird things. Some viruses are nothing more than mere annoyances that display cute, or not-so-cute, messages. Others can be very destructive. They wait until a particular date and then go on a rampage and destroy files. Sometimes they erase the entire contents of a person's hard drive.

To keep your system free of viruses, there are a handful of things you should do:

- Back up your files regularly. (If your computer is infected with a virus, you must remember to disinfect the restored files.)

- Never boot your computer with a floppy disk that you
  haven't scanned and disinfected first. (When you scan
  your computer with an antivirus program, you search
  your computer's memory and program files for viruses.
  If a virus is found, the antivirus program removes the
  virus from your computer.)

- Always disinfect every file you download from a BBS,
  copy from a floppy disk, or copy from a network drive
  before running it on your computer.

- Install an antivirus program, like Norton Antivirus, and
  use the memory-resident virus-spotting portion of the
  program at all times.

Norton Antivirus scans your files and your directories whenever your computer is turned on. It can also scan each floppy
disk for viruses before files are copied onto your computer.
Should a virus be detected, Norton AntiVirus can quickly
repair infected files. **Norton AntiVirus.** Symantec Corporation,
10201 Torre Avenue, Cupertino, CA 95014, 800-441-7234.

Bells and Whistles for Your Next Computer

When you're ready to buy a new computer, read this section
for the list of the bells and whistles that I recommend you buy.
As far as brand names go, there are many good ones. But I feel
that the quality of service the manufacturer or computer store
offers is of primary importance. (I've been buying all of my
computers from a little store on the northwest side of Chicago,
Ernie's Office Machines. Rich Barkoff, who owns the place, has
always given me great service and has *forgotten* more about
computers than I'll ever know.) I feel that the quality of the
computer store is even more meaningful than low price,
because when you've got a question or have a problem, you
want to be able to talk with someone who can help you.

That said, here are the things I would get in a new computer if
money weren't an issue. (But since it probably is, you'll just
have decide which features are more or less important to you.)

Buy a super-fast computer

Today it's a Pentium or Power PC; tomorrow it'll be the P6; beyond that I don't have the slightest idea. You'll never be disappointed when you buy the fastest computer that's currently available.

Add lots of memory

Today you need a minimum of 8MB just to get your computer to run. If you're going to purchase a Pentium, you should get 16MB, or even 32MB of memory.

Include a huge hard drive

Five years ago, a 40MB hard drive was satisfactory. Today, you should get at least a 500MB hard drive, and for just a little more money you can get a 1000MB (gigabyte) hard drive.

Put in a fast video card

Get a video card with at least 4MB of memory. Your graphics programs, CD-ROMS, and games will fly across your screen.

Get a big monitor

When we started using computers, we had these itty bitty black-and-white (or was it green?) monitors. Today there are 15-, 17-, or 21-inch monitors that display 16 million colors. Treat yourself to either a 17- or 21-inch monitor. You'll thank yourself for it.

For fun, install a fast CD-ROM

The first CD-ROMs were slow, and it took a lot of time to transfer information from the CD-ROM to the computer. Along came double-speed CD-ROM drives, then triple-speed, and now even quadruple-speed CD-ROM drives. If you plan on using your CD-ROM, get a triple-speed. If you plan on using it a lot, get a quadruple-speed CD-ROM.

Don't forget a sound card with high quality speakers

If you're going to be using your CD-ROM, you need a good sound card and great speakers. Your system should sound as good as the graphics look.

To communicate with the outside world, you need a high speed modem

Three years ago, we were happy with 2400 bps (bits per second) modems. Last year 14,400 bps modems were the rage, and now everybody's starting to use 28,800 bps modems. Buy the fastest modem that's available. Your computer is the gateway to the world, and your modem is your key.

Protect yourself with a backup tape drive

Backing up your hard drive just makes good sense. With an automatic backup system, the whole process is very easy, and should something happen to your computer, you'll be able to restore any lost or damaged files in almost no time at all.

Other Equipment for Your Home Office

You need more than just a computer and telephone for your home office. You should consider purchasing a fax machine, a modem, and a good printer if you are serious about making your office at home.

You need a fax machine

You've got to have a fax machine today. There's no way around it. It's just so much quicker and faster to fax a copy of a document to a person instead of mailing it. (You can fax directly from your computer without ever handling a piece of paper; I discuss WinFax Pro later in this part.)

Brother International makes a complete line of fax machines for the home and the corporate office. **Brother International Corporation.** 200 Cottontail Lane, Somerset, NJ 08875. For the name of your nearest Brother dealer, call 800-284-4357.

Let your fingers do the walking . . . with a modem

If you really want to expand your horizons, increase your knowledge, improve your productivity, and give yourself access to an almost unlimited amount of information, you need to attach a modem to your computer. A modem gives you the opportunity not only to communicate with other people using your computer, it also gives you the capability to send and receive e-mail messages and computer files, access on-line information services, search thousands of databases, and share information with people who have similar interests on bulletin board services (BBSs). And best of all, you can use it to dial your phone for you.

Hayes Microcomputer Products has developed and sold more modems and communications software for personal computers than any other company in the world. Their widely implemented technologies have given rise to the phrase "Hayes compatible" that is prevalent in virtually any modem advertisement you see. Hayes makes a number of different modems that are designed specifically for use at home or in the office. **Hayes Modems.** Hayes Microcomputer Products, Inc., P.O. Box 105203, Atlanta, GA 30348. Call 404-840-9200 for a catalog, price list, and the name of your nearest Hayes dealer.

You need a good printer

One of the reasons you're able to work out of the home and be so extremely productive at the same time is the personal computer. With today's super-fast machines and powerful software, you can produce the kinds of letters, documents, presentations, and proposals in hours that used to take a group of people the better part of a day.

But the creation of the work inside the computer is only the first part of the process. The second part is getting it to look good on paper. And if you want it to look as good on paper as it does on your computer screen, you need to have a good printer.

Brother International makes a complete line of printers for the home and the office. Their newest line of laser printers — the HL-630, HL-645, HL-655 — offer high-quality printing at affordable prices. (The first two models have a 16 MHz microprocessor and 512KB, and 1MB, of RAM respectively. The HL-655 has a 25 MHz microprocessor with 2MB RAM.) With Brother's "Straight Paper Path" design you can print on a wide variety of paper stocks and sizes — from 3" x 5" index cards, to letter envelopes, to legal sized paper. All three printers print at 6 pages per minute.

If you need a high-end laser printer, the HL-1260 is a phenom-enal machine! It's designed for the person who needs high-quality text and graphics output, network connectivity, and the capability to handle complex printing tasks easily and effortlessly. The HL-1260 is fast. It prints at the rate of 12 pages per minute at a resolution of 600 DPI (dots per inch). (For graphical output, you can increase the resolution to 1200 DPI.) Printed text and graphics look so good that you would think the printed document was created by a "professional" printer.

The HL-1260 is driven by a super-fast 32-bit, 20 MHz RISC processor and comes with 2MB RAM that can be easily upgraded to 26MB. It even comes with a 500-sheet, multipur-pose paper tray. And if you need a color printer, Brother's HS-1PS has a lot of printing power.

I've been using the same Brother printer for more than five years now (not the HL-1260; it's brand new) — and have written four books with it. Day after day, it's done what it was designed to do. I turn it on, and it prints, and prints, and prints. The only time it stops is when it's run out of paper or the toner cartridge needs to be replaced. It's been a depend-able workhorse.

Brother International makes a complete line of printers for the home and the corporate office. **Brother International Corpo-ration.** 200 Cottontail Lane, Somerset, NJ 08875. For the name of your nearest Brother dealer, call 800-284-4357.

Software That Will Save You Time

The following is a summary of the software that I use every day. I find that these programs save me time and make me much more efficient. (In my best-selling *Winning the Fight Between You and Your Desk,* I review more than 150 computer programs that can help you become more productive.)

WordPerfect

I've been using WordPerfect products for years, and I think they're great! I wrote my first three books with WordPerfect 5.1 for DOS, and this book was written with WordPerfect 6.1 for Windows. The productivity-improving features in WordPerfect 6.1 enable me to spend all of my time and energy writing. I don't have to be concerned with the layout or format of the text because WordPerfect does it for me. WordPerfect 6.1 for Windows has increased my writing efficiency by at least 50 percent over WordPerfect 5.1 for DOS. **WordPerfect 6.1 for Windows.** WordPerfect Novell Applications Group, 1555 N. Technology Way, Orem, UT 84957, 800-451-5151.

ACT!

ACT! runs my life. It's the first computer program I turn on in the morning and the last one I turn off in the evening. By using it, I have been able to automate all of my follow-up tasks — my calls, meetings, and to-dos — and it has improved my daily productivity three- or fourfold. (Somehow I think you already know that I like ACT! I'm even writing *ACT! For Dummies,* which will be published in the summer of 1995.) **ACT!** Symantec Corporation, 10201 Torre Avenue, Cupertino, CA 95014, 800-441-7234.

Quicken

Quicken has enabled me to automate all of my financial record keeping. It keeps track of my bank balances; it prints my checks; it categorizes all of my financial transactions (my tax preparation costs have gone down by more than 50 percent); and it helps me stay on top of all my saving and investment programs. For many people, Quicken has been a reason to go out and buy a computer, and I heartily agree. **Quicken.** Intuit, P.O. Box 3014, Menlo Park, CA 94026, 800-624-6095.

QuickBooks

If you run a small business, you need an easy-to-use accounting program, and Intuit's QuickBooks can help you take care of all your financial record keeping. You can use it to write your checks, keep your check register, create and print your invoices, show the aging of your accounts receivable, and keep track of your accounts payable and balance sheet — your assets, liabilities, and net worth. **QuickBooks.** Intuit, P.O. Box 3014, Menlo Park, CA 94026, 800-624-6095.

WordPerfect Presentations

WordPerfect Presentations is an easy to use graphics and drawing program. I use it to create and design charts, graphs, drawings, and illustrations that are used in my slide shows, overhead transparencies, and handouts. I even used WordPerfect Presentations to create the screen shots of the computer programs that were used throughout this book. **WordPerfect Presentations.** WordPerfect Novell Applications Group, 1555 N. Technology Way, Orem, UT 84957, 800-451-5151.

UnInstaller

Removing old or unused programs from Windows can be a bit tricky because these programs put references to themselves all over the place. They may create .INI files for themselves (don't ask me what an .INI file is, because I don't know) and add a few lines about the program in files named SYSTEM.INI or WIN.INI (files that are needed to run Windows, but no one has been able to adequately explain to me what they are, why they're there, or what they do).

MicroHelp's UnInstaller removes the program's files, searches your computer's entire hard drive looking for all these miscellaneous .INI things, and then gives you the opportunity to delete them, one at a time. UnInstaller is a great utility program. **UnInstaller.** MicroHelp, Inc., 439 Shallowford Industrial Parkway, Marietta, GA 30066, 800-922-3383.

Norton Backup and the Colorado Jumbo Tape Drive

Five years ago, it was easy to back up your hard drive onto floppy disks. But how do you back up a 250MB, 500MB, or 1000MB (1 *gigabyte!*) drive? The only way you can do it is with a cassette tape drive and backup software.

I've found the Norton Backup software and the Colorado Backup Tape Drive to be a great combination. I've automated the whole process, and it's made my life really easy. Every afternoon at 6:00 p.m., the backup program automatically turns itself on and backs up all the files that have changed since my last full backup. About once a week, I do a full backup of my entire hard drive.

If you're not backing up your computer on a regular basis, you're taking an unnecessary risk, because sooner or later, something bad is going to happen and you're going to lose some, or all, of your data. It's happened to me more than once, and Norton Backup has been both a lifesaver and a huge time-saver.

Norton Backup. Symantec Corporation, 10201 Torre Avenue, Cupertino, CA 95014, 800-441-7234. **Jumbo Tape Backup System.** Colorado Memory Systems, Inc., 800 S. Taft Avenue, Loveland, CO 80537, 800-451-4523. Colorado Memory Systems makes many different sizes and types of tape drives.

Norton Utilities

And speaking of lifesavers, I think everyone should have a copy of Norton Utilities. Norton Utilities is a collection of utility programs that are designed to keep your computer's hard drive in tip-top shape. If there's a problem, Norton Utilities has a utility that can fix it; if you were to lose some information as a result of that problem, you can use a Restore Utility that's designed to recover damaged Lotus 1-2-3, Symphony, Excel, Quattro Pro, dBASE, and WordPerfect files. **Norton Utilities.** Symantec Corporation, 10201 Torre Avenue, Cupertino, CA 95014, 800-441-7234.

Seiko Smart Label Printer Pro

How do you print a single label? Good question, isn't it? Somehow, I don't think that laser printers were designed to print a single label. Typing a label on one of those old fashioned things — an electric typewriter — was always a time-consuming task.

But printing a label with the Seiko Smart Label Printer Pro is easy. The SLP Printer Pro attaches to the serial port of your computer and prints labels from a roll, one at a time, instead of from a sheet. Seiko has even developed software that searches for the address in your letter and then automatically prints the label, with bar codes, for you. What could be easier? I use mine every day and find that it's a great productivity-improvement tool. Now it's time to get rid of that old type-writer. **Smart Label Printer Pro.** Seiko Instruments USA Inc., 1130 Ringwood Court, San Jose, CA 95131, 800-888-0817.

Bootcon

The following may be a little technical, but please forgive me, because it's important. You may not be aware of this, but when you turn on your computer, you load a lot of different *device drivers* — little programs that run devices such as your sound card, CD-ROM drive, flatbed scanner, handheld scanner, and lots of other miscellaneous things — into your computer's memory. Now, this is okay if you're using the sound card, CD-ROM, and all those other things all the time. But if you're not, you're wasting valuable system resources, which can cause your whole system to run slower. That's where Bootcon comes in.

Bootcon is a utility program that enables you to select different system configurations so that you can decide which device drivers, and other things, you want to load into memory when you turn on your computer. **Bootcon.** Modular Software Systems, 25825 104th Avenue SE, Suite 208, Kent, WA 98031, 800-438-3930.

SuperPrint

I don't know how you feel, but I think it's a waste of time to sit at a computer and not be able to use it. This happens to me every time I print a document with the Windows print manager. After the print manager starts sending information to the printer, it takes control of the computer and won't give it back. In the meantime, I have nothing to do except sit there, twiddle my thumbs, and feel frustrated. With Zenographics's SuperPrint, I don't have to sit and wait any more. I can continue working while SuperPrint prints.

After I press the print button, SuperPrint collects all the information that my printer needs in just a few moments. It then returns control of my computer to me so that I can continue working while it sends the printing information to the printer. **SuperPrint.** Zenographics, 4 Executive Circle, Irvine, CA 92714, 800-566-7468.

WinFax Pro

One of the biggest time-saving and productivity-improving inventions in the last decade has been the fax machine. And although fax machines have made it possible to send and receive information in an instant, most of us still follow a cumbersome procedure: We print hard copies of that letter or document that we just created in the computer. Then we walk to the fax machine, insert the document into the paper feeder, and send the fax, assuming that the machine isn't already in use. If it is, we wait.

And what happens when someone sends *you* a fax? Unless the machine is nearby, you have no way of knowing whether a fax has been received, so it may sit there for hours before you get it.

With WinFax Pro, you can send and receive all of your faxes directly from your computer without ever touching a piece of paper. There's no more walking back and forth to the fax machine; no more standing in line waiting for the machine to become available; and no more greasy, curly paper to deal with. And best of all, when you receive a fax, you're notified instantly and can review it on-screen or print it. If you send a lot of faxes, WinFax Pro can save you a lot of time. **WinFax Pro.** Delrina Technology Inc., 6830 Via Del Oro, San Jose, CA 95119, 800-268-6082.

HyperACCESS

If you need communications software, Hilgraeve's HyperACCESS is very easy to use. It makes the process of transferring information from your computer to someone else's a breeze, and it supports hundreds of modems. And its virus-detection program prevents viruses from entering your computer as you're downloading files. **HyperACCESS.** Hilgraeve, Inc., 111 Conant Avenue, Monroe, MI 48161; 800-826-2760.

You can improve your productivity by upgrading your software. Whenever the developers of your favorite programs release new versions, you should go out and buy copies. (They'll let you know about it because you'll get a postcard in the mail every day for at least six months.)

Make the Telephone Your Friend

If you work at home, using your phone is even more important in your everyday business tasks. Therefore, the more you know about how to use your phone to your advantage, the more productive you will be. This section contains helpful tips for more effective phone conversations.

How do you come across on the phone?

I know you've been using the phone since you were about four years old, but have you ever thought about how you come across on the phone? And no matter how good you are on the phone, you can still work on improving your telephone techniques.

Your feelings and emotions come across loud and clear

Have you ever been really angry about something and then picked up the phone to call someone else — who had nothing to do with the source of your anger — and then let this poor, unsuspecting soul have it? I know that I have, and usually I felt so bad about it afterwards that I often called to apologize for my rude behavior.

Well, whatever you're feeling inside — happy, sad, joyful, depressed — is reflected in your voice as soon as you pick up the receiver and start talking to someone. If you speak with an individual face to face, he or she sees — and responds to — your nonverbal messages, such as your facial expressions, eye movements, and posture, as well as the gestures you make with your hands, arms, and legs.

And when you're on the telephone, even though the party at the other end of the phone can't see these nonverbal gestures, your attitudes, feelings, thoughts, and opinions are immediately transmitted by the tone of your voice, its pitch, the speed at which you talk, and even your choice of words. So whenever you're speaking on the phone, you're going to be conveying a message. It may be one that indicates that you're happy to talk with them and want the conversation to continue, or it could be one that indicates that you're bored, disinterested, and have a desire to be doing something else at this very moment.

Keep a smile on your face

You may find this hard to believe, but you'll come across much better on the phone if you can keep a smile on your face and project that smile onto the person you are talking with. People warm up to you when you meet them face-to-face and smile, and they'll do the same thing when you smile at them through the phone.

For many years, I've kept a mirror in front of me as a reminder to smile when I'm on the phone. It helps me sound more friendly and open. My suggestion to you: Put a small mirror on your desk so that you can watch yourself smile when you're on the phone.

Be enthusiastic

Have you ever had conversations with people who sound as if they've just come back from a funeral or a wake? They talk in a very dull and dreary monotone. Their tone of voice is completely void of life and energy, and this is when they're calling to tell you *good* news! I don't know about you, but when I get these kinds of calls I want to crawl under the desk and hide.

So when you get on the phone, put some life, energy, and emotion in your voice. Don't be afraid to express yourself verbally and emotionally. Make your voice so interesting that the person at the other end of the phone wants to hear what it is that you have to say.

Have fun when you're on the phone. Be yourself. Let your sense of humor show through and don't forget to laugh. Laughter can be a great icebreaker.

Always take a deep breath before you begin to speak. When you have air in your lungs, your voice has more depth and power.

Practice your telephone techniques

I know that up until now you've probably never given a moment's thought to your telephone technique, but it can be a real ear opener when you record some of your calls and hear yourself as others hear you. You would probably be amazed at how many times you said things such as "you know," "and," and "um," during each sentence. Then there are the sentences that you start but never complete. And finally, there's your voice itself. What does it sound like? Is it energetic and enthusiastic, or does it come across like a limp wash rag?

But no matter what your voice sounds like today, with just a little bit of practice on your part, it's very easy to improve your ability to express yourself and communicate with other people over the phone. After you play back the tape of yourself speaking on the phone and hear what you're saying and how you're saying it, you'll become much more aware of the speech habits you've picked up. You can start working on breaking those habits so that you speak with more clarity. The first thing that you'll become aware of is how many times you say such things as "you know"or "um." In no time at all, you'll be able to stop yourself from saying these things.

What is the purpose of the call?

Being aware of how you sound and come across on the phone is one thing, but knowing why you are making the call is another. In today's high-pressure business world, we don't have the luxury of wasting time. One of the biggest time wasters of all is the phone call that has no apparent purpose. Whenever you're about to make a call, you should always ask yourself these questions:

- Why am I making this call?

- What information do I want?

- What information do I wish to convey?

- How much of the other person's time do I need?

- What do I do if the other person is not there and I get his or her secretary, assistant, or the receptionist? (I talk about this situation later in this section.)

- What do I do if I get the other person's voice mail? (I discuss voice mail later in this part.)

Here are some tips that can help you to prepare for your phone calls:

- Make a list of the items that you want to discuss with the person.

- Arrange the sequence of the items so that the most important items will be discussed first.

- Have the files or other papers to which you'll need to refer at your fingertips.

- If this is a very important or difficult call and you're not sure exactly what you want to say or how you want to say it, write everything out on a piece of paper. A word of caution here: When you get the other person on the phone, have your notes available for reference, but don't read them.

 Spend a few moments thinking about and preparing yourself for each call before you make it. Treat each call as if it were a face-to-face business meeting.

When you know that it's going to take you an hour to go through all the things that you've got to talk with a person about, schedule a conference call so that the two of you can block out the time on your calendars. You should also let the other person know in advance of that call what you're going to be talking about so that he or she can be thoroughly prepared.

If you're calling to schedule an appointment, always offer two different times on different days. You could say something like, "Are you free on Monday afternoon, or would Tuesday morning be better?" This question changes the flow of the conversation from *if* the person will see you to *when* the person will see you.

Beat the odds

Because everyone's so busy, it's almost impossible to reach a person on the phone the first time you call. As a result, everyone ends up playing telephone tag. You know how the game's played: I call you and leave a message, and then you call me and leave a message; and this goes on and on. Eventually we talk, or we get tied up with other things and forget about it.

But there are a few facts about the telephone that you should be aware of. The chance of actually reaching a person on the first try is less than 20 percent. In other words, there's only a one in five chance that when you call a specific person, he or she will be available to take your call. And there's an 80 percent probability that the person you hope to talk to will be tied up in a meeting — or on the phone. So, if you want to reach an individual on the phone, you've got to be persistent and should expect to call at least five times.

Don't leave messages

If there's someone you want to speak to, it's your job to track him or her down. And just because you left a message doesn't mean that you'll be called back — your call may be much more important to you than it is to the other person — and even if you are called back, the odds aren't very good that you'll be there to take that return call.

So when you need to speak to someone, here are some techniques you can use to increase your odds of getting through.

- **Work with the secretary.** If the person you're trying to reach is in meetings, try to find out when he or she will be out of them and ask if that would be a good time to call. If he or she is on the phone, ask the secretary for an idea of how long the call will last. Then ask whether it would be better for you to be put on hold for a few moments or call back in fifteen minutes. When the secretary says, "Let me take your number and I'll have So'n'so call you back," just say, "Thank you, I'll call back later," because the person *probably* won't be calling you back.

- **Get a direct number.** Try to get the person's direct number so that you can bypass the secretary, administrative assistant, or switchboard entirely.

- **Call early in the morning.** Many business people are at their desks as early as 7 a.m. each morning. So ask the secretary if the person you're trying to reach comes in early in the morning.

- **Call after work.** Many people are also working long after 5 p.m., so perhaps you can get through if you call after 5:30 p.m.

- **Call during lunch.** Many people work through lunch — or eat at their desks. So give it a shot and try your luck by calling at 12:30 p.m.

Calling is another area where ACT! can really improve your productivity. First off, you can't lose track of a call. If you don't reach an individual today, ACT! automatically rolls it over to tomorrow. Second, when you're told that someone's out of town for two weeks, you just click the pop-up calendar and change the date of the call. In two weeks, that person's name appears again. And third, you'll love ACT!'s alarm. When you're told that someone's tied up in a meeting for about another 20 minutes, just set the alarm, and in 20 minutes you'll be reminded to make the call.

Take notes of the conversation

When you speak to a person on the phone, you should keep notes of your conversation and place them in the file you keep for that person. Though you may be blessed with a phenomenal memory, with the passage of time, it becomes difficult to re-member exactly what a person said and when he or she said it.

When you get off the phone, you should write a brief note to summarize what was said, who's got to do what, and when it's supposed to be done. This note should be put in the appropriate file. If there's work to do, it should be added to your Master List.

Note taking is another area where ACT! excels. After the call, you can enter your notes in the person's notepad, and if there's work to do, you can enter that item on the Task List. The whole thing takes just a few moments. No muss. No fuss. And no pieces of paper to file.

Dialing for dollars

If you're in a business where it's important for you to spend time on the phone, you should know that there are certain times during the day when you're most likely to find people sitting at their desks and available to take your call. As a general rule, people are usually in their offices from 9 a.m. to 11 a.m. and from about 2 p.m. to 4 p.m. You should always block out those times on your calendar so that you can get on the telephone and make your calls.

What do you do when your phone rings?

Up until now, we've been discussing how you can get through to people when you're calling them. But what do you do when *your* phone rings? You need some techniques that will help you with your incoming calls, and that's what you're going to get in the following section.

You don't have to answer every call

Just because the phone rings doesn't mean that you have to answer it. Whenever the phone rings, it's an interruption. And if you're in the midst of doing something important, the last thing you want to do is allow yourself to be interrupted.

 It's okay to let your voice-mail system or answering machine take the call. If you answer the phone every time it rings, you'll never get any work done.

 Use the screening feature of your voice-mail system to see who is calling. You can let the machine answer the phone. If it's important, you can pick up the receiver. And if it isn't important? Keep working!

Who's calling?

When you do answer the phone, you need to know the answers to two questions: "Who's calling?" and "What do you want?" (You can be a bit more *tactful* and less blunt when you're speaking with the other person, but you need to know who the other caller is and why he or she is calling.)

If the caller doesn't identify him or herself, or is very vague about why he or she is calling, it's okay to say, "Good-bye!" and hang up the phone.

If you do want to talk to the caller, you should ask, "How much time is this going to take?" If the call will just take a few minutes, you may wish to have the conversation now; otherwise, you should schedule a time to talk later in the day. Most important, you want to avoid spending 30 minutes on a call when you should be completing your important work.

Get rid of cold callers

It seems that whenever I pick up the phone, there's someone at the other end trying to sell me medical insurance, penny stocks on the Vancouver Stock Exchange, a new long-distance phone service, or something else that I don't need or want. You can always tell who these people are because they all start their calls in the same way:

Caller: *"Is Mr. Mayer there?"*

Me: *"Yes, this is he."*

Caller: *"How are you today?"*

When the caller says, "How are you today?" you *know* that someone's trying to sell you something.

If you let these people get started with their sales pitch, it's difficult to get rid of them — you don't want to be rude — because they're always asking you to answer questions that are impossible to disagree with, such as: "How would you like an investment that has a very high rate of return with no risk?" The best thing you can do is to cut them short and just say "I'm not interested!" and hang up the phone.

Now, the two or three minutes that it takes to answer an unsolicited call may not sound like much. But multiply that by several dozen calls per day, and you've eaten up a huge chunk of time that you should have spent working on your high-priority projects. (And you wonder why you never get anything done.)

Don't say to salespeople, "I can't talk to you now; just send me something in the mail." First of all, you don't need any more junk mail. And second, after they send you their materials, they're going to start calling again to ask whether you've had a chance to look at them.

Watch your socializing

I know that it's nice to chat with friends, but if you do it throughout the day, it's a very easy way to lose track of a lot of time. Just add five minutes of socializing to each of your calls, and by the end of the day, you could easily lose an hour or two. And let's not forget about those "five minute" calls that end up lasting an hour. So try to keep the number of your social calls at a reasonable level and be aware of how much time you're spending on each of them.

No one has enough time during the course of the workday, and one of the ways you can give yourself more time is to minimize the number and length of your social calls. As an alternative to talking over the phone, perhaps you should meet for lunch or dinner.

Thank the caller for complaining

A person who takes the time to complain is a person who wants to continue doing business with you. By complaining, these people are telling you what it is they want or need from you. When people call to complain, don't become defensive or argumentative. Just thank them for telling you what it is that they're unhappy with and then say something like, "Thank you for taking the time to call. I'm glad you brought that to my attention. We'll do our best to solve this problem for you."

Coping with difficult telephone conversations

I don't know how often this happens to you, but now and then, I find that I've gotten myself into a difficult phone conversation and am having a hard time trying to get myself out of it. Sometimes things just aren't going my way, and other times, my mind's coming up blank. So here are a few tips for dealing with these types of situations:

- **Put the caller on hold.** When you need a moment to regroup yourself or to get the other person to calm down, just put the caller on hold for a few moments. When you get back on the line, you'll be better prepared to continue your verbal jousting.

- **Hang up on yourself.** If things aren't going well during a phone conversation, just hang up — in mid-sentence — on yourself. The other person will think that there was just a glitch in the line. Here's how you do it: While you're saying something important, just hang up on yourself, right in the middle of your sentence. By the time the conversation resumes, you will have given yourself a few minutes to think about the topic of your conversation. (Depending upon the dynamics of the situation, you'll have to decide whether you want to call back immediately, wait a few minutes and then call back, or wait for the other person to call you.)

Getting the Most out of Voice Mail

Every business in America now has voice mail, or at least it seems that way. If you use voice mail effectively, you can reduce the time it takes to exchange information and can make yourself more productive.

Why use voice mail?

The telephone has one terrible shortcoming: Both the caller and the callee must be present at each end of the telephone for a conversation to take place. But statistics tell us that almost 80 percent of all business calls are not completed on the first attempt. Of these calls, at least half of them are one-way transfers of information, and almost two-thirds of all phone calls are less important than the work they interrupt. So here are some reasons that you should be using voice mail:

- Voice mail enables you to share information without actually speaking to the other person.

- Voice mail lets you communicate in non-real time. You don't have to wait until noon, rise at 6 a.m., or stay awake until midnight to call someone on the other coast, in the Far East, or in Europe.

- Voice mail messages are usually much shorter than the actual telephone call.

- Voice mail is available 24 hours a day, seven days a week. (Some systems are even designed so that when a voice mail message is received after normal business hours or on the weekend, the system calls the recipient at home to inform him or her that a voice mail message has been received.)

- Voice mail can reduce the length of time that you're stuck on hold.

A recent survey conducted by the Voice Messaging Educational Committee of Morris Plains, NJ found that 58 percent of the callers surveyed would rather leave a message on voice mail than with a secretary or receptionist. Of these:

- Nearly half feared that a secretary or receptionist would lose some of the details while taking down the message.

- Eighteen percent felt that more detail could be conveyed through voice mail.

- Sixteen percent preferred delivering the information in their own speaking style.

Recording your message

Whether you're using an answering machine or have a sophisticated voice-mail system, here are some thoughts about recording your outgoing message.

Some people like to record a basic message once and never make any changes to it. Others like to record a new message every day so that they can leave a detailed schedule of their activities for the caller. The latter type of message is very helpful to both the caller and the callee because it helps improve the odds of the caller and the callee being able to reach each other since the caller knows when the callee is expected to be in the office and behind the desk. Let me give you a few examples of very good voice-mail messages:

> *Hello, this is Fred Smith. It's Friday, January 20th, and I'll be out of the office all day today and all day on Monday. Please leave me your name, number, and a brief message. I will be checking in for messages throughout the day.*

> *Hello, this is Carol Collins, of the Building Managers Association. It's Tuesday, August 22. I'm sorry I missed your*

call. I am out of the office today. If you're calling in regard to completion of the US Industrial survey and you need some extra time, please leave me a message as to when you think you can send it to me. If you have any questions that you need answered today, please call Sherry Ackerman in Dallas. Her number is 123-456-7890. If this call is in regard to other matters, please leave me a message and I'll get back to you as soon as I can.

Hello, this is Kelly Green. It's Monday, October 17, and I'm in the office today; however, I'm going to be tied up in meetings for most of it. I will check in later, though, so please leave a message and I'll get back to you as soon as I possibly can.

Here are some things you should remember when you record your voice-mail message:

- Your message should be informative, courteous, and brief, and should always encourage the caller to leave a message.

- Smile before you start speaking, and the warmth of your smile will come through in your voice, and you'll leave a friendlier greeting.

- To put some life, energy, and enthusiasm into your voice-mail message, get up from your chair, stretch for a moment, get the blood in your body circulating, and then record your message. You don't want your message to sound as if you recorded it just before you had to go to a funeral.

- When you record your voice-mail message, always speak slowly, distinctly, and clearly.

- If you're going to ask people to leave you messages, you've got to check your messages throughout the day and must be diligent about returning your calls.

- After you have recorded your voice-mail message, call yourself up to listen to how it sounds. Does it have enough energy and enthusiasm? Is it short and concise? Does it say what you want it to say? If not, record it again.

Tips for leaving voice-mail messages

Recording a voice-mail message is one thing, but leaving messages is an entirely different, and more important, subject. In today's business world, almost everyone has voice mail. So whenever you make a call, you should be prepared to leave a message. Therefore, you should think about what you want to say and how you want to say it — *before* you make the call. Here are some tips on how to leave better voice mail messages:

- Don't start leaving your message until you hear the machine beep. (I know that almost everybody should know this, but you would be surprised at the number of people who start talking before the outgoing message is finished.)

- Before you start speaking, take a deep breath so that your lungs are full of air. This action will give your voice more depth and power.

- When you speak, speak slowly, clearly, and concisely so that the person can understand what you're saying. Don't swallow your words.

- Make your voice sound interesting. Speak with enthusiasm. Put some energy into your voice.

- When you leave your name, in addition to saying it, you should spell it out. ("This is Jeffrey Mayer, M-A-Y-E-R.")

- Always give your phone number twice, once at the beginning of the call and again at the end of the call. Even if you know that the other person has your phone number, he or she may be calling in for messages and may not have your number handy.

- When you leave your message, state the most important points first, with the lesser points following.

- If you're including your mailing address, speak slowly and spell out the name of your street and city after you say the address. ("50 East Bellevue Place, B-E-L-L-E-V-U-E, Chicago, Illinois.")

- Leave a specific time, or a window of time, when you'll be available for the person to call you back. For example: "I'll be in my office, and available, tomorrow morning"; or "I'm always in my office every afternoon after 2:00."

Be energetic and enthusiastic. Let your personality brighten the other person's day.

What if my voice-mail messages aren't returned?

If you leave voice-mail messages several times with a person, and they aren't returned, try to talk with the person's assistant, someone else in the department, or the receptionist to find out if the person you're calling is in town and available. If you're unable to reach this person, try to get the name of someone else you can speak with.

After you've called someone a few times and have left voice-mail messages that haven't been returned, try to reach the person's assistant or someone else in the department. Find out when the person you're trying to contact may be available to take your call. Don't sit around waiting for a return call that won't be forthcoming.

But I get too many messages

One of the biggest complaints I get about voice mail is that people get too many messages, and it takes too long to listen to them. Here are some tips that can help you deal with this problem:

- Increase the playback speed of your calls. When you listen to your messages, speed them up so that you can get through them quickly. (This feature may not be available on all voice-mail systems or home answering machines.)

- Limit the length of time for each message. If you've got long-winded people, limit the length of time that a person can leave a message to 60, 90, or 120 seconds at most. (When you record your message, tell callers that they have only 60 seconds to leave their messages.)

- Limit the number of calls your voice mail box or answering machine can hold. I know this action may sound like it's defeating the purpose of the voice-mail system. But if you're getting too many calls, try limiting the number of calls that your voice mail box can hold. When your box is full, the caller will be told something like: "This voice mail box is full." Now the caller will have to call someone else, call back later, or send a letter or e-mail message.

- If you get a message for something that doesn't pertain to you, transfer the message to the person who is responsible.

Taking care of business

After you get these messages, you've got to do something with them. So here are a few suggestions:

- If there's work to do, you should note it on your Master List or put it into ACT!.

- If the information is important, you should take notes on a big piece of paper — one note per page — and put it in the appropriate file. (Don't forget to date your papers.)

- When you're finished listening to your messages, erase them.

You Should Be on CompuServe

One of the biggest complaints that people who work at home have is that they don't have enough interaction with other people, and they don't have the ability to ask coworkers or colleagues questions. CompuServe solves many of these problems. CompuServe is the oldest and largest of all the commercial on-line services with almost 3 million members. If there's anything you need or want, you can probably find it on CompuServe.

User groups or forums

There are more than 2600 forums on CompuServe.

You have got to join the Working From Home forum on Compu-Serve! The Working From Home forum was founded on Compu-Serve by Paul and Sarah Edwards, authors of the best-selling book *Working from Home*. The forum has thousands of active members and is a great way to make friends and find answers to questions. (To join the Working From Home forum, type GO WORK.)

Bulletin boards

In each forum there's a bulletin board where you can ask questions or post messages. You can also read the messages — and the responses to those messages — that other members have posted. (Post your question at 10 p.m. in the evening, and you'll probably have a half-dozen responses by 7 a.m. the next morning; the responses could be from anywhere in the world.)

File library

There is also a file library of all sorts of useful, and not so useful, computer files which you can browse or download to your own computer.

Talk to people in real time

You have the ability to have on-line conversations with other forum members in real time.

Databases

If you're doing research, you can browse a host of databases for newspaper and magazine articles on every imaginable subject, all from the comfort of your home or office. When you find something that's of interest, just download it into your computer.

E-mail

E-mail is a big part of CompuServe. You can send e-mail messages to anyone who is a CompuServe member and to anyone who has an e-mail address anywhere in the world. As a part of sending e-mail, you can also attach computer files to your e-mail message. You can transfer huge amounts of information in just a few moments of time. Sending e-mail is much more effective than sending someone a fax. (The book you are holding in your hands was written electronically. I wrote my text in WordPerfect 6.1 for Windows, saved the file in Microsoft Word format, and sent it via CompuServe to my editor, Tim Gallan. Tim made editorial changes in Word for the Mac, saved the file in WordPerfect format, and e-mailed it back to me. We never handled a piece of paper.)

Get answers to technical computer questions

If you have technical questions about your computer or your software, almost every vendor in the country is a member of CompuServe. You can go into the vendor's forum and send and receive e-mail messages from other people who use the same hardware or software that you do. And you can often communicate with people from the company's technical support department.

Before you buy your next computer or upgrade your software, go into the vendor's forum, or to the user's group, and post a message that asks about a certain product that you are thinking about purchasing. Within a day you'll know if you should or shouldn't make your purchase. It's also a lot of fun reading all of the other messages that people have left on the bulletin board. Nobody's shy on CompuServe.

Here are some other miscellaneous things you can do on CompuServe:

- **Who is a potential customer?** If you're selling a product or a service, CompuServe offers you many opportunities to come into contact with a potential buyer. And when you're looking for a specific product, someone on CompuServe probably has exactly what you need.

- **What's the weather like?** If you're going on a trip and want to know what the weather will be — anywhere in the United States or in the world — just type in the name of the city and click OK. Within a few moments, you'll be able to read the National Weather Services's local weather forecasts and look at the weather maps.

- **What's happening in the news?** For those of you who are news junkies, you can read the latest stories straight off the Associated Press wire service. You no longer have to wait till the top of the hour to find out what's going on in the world. You can read tomorrow morning's headlines now. (And if you want the latest sports scores, you can get those off the AP also.)

For more information about CompuServe you can write or call **CompuServe.** 5000 Arlington Centre Blvd., Columbus, OH 43220, 800-848-8990. (After you join CompuServe, you should get a copy of *CompuServe For Dummies.*)

I posted a message in several of the CompuServe forums asking people "How do you use CompuServe to save time?" One person wrote this message back to me within a day:

> Where CompuServe really excels, Jeff, is in eliminating the need to "reinvent the wheel." For example, a couple of days ago a TV producer in Seattle posted a message on this forum stating that he was trying to make an underwater housing for a small, lipstick-sized camera. He asked if any forum members had experience or suggestions in such an undertaking.

He has already received several replies, and I noticed in the download file in which I found your message that a forum member has provided him with step-by-step, inch-by-inch directions. These forums allow us to share a vast pool of experience with many other people, pools into which we can reach with just a few keystrokes. Never before in the history of mankind has it been so easy for so many to work together.

The Final Frontier: The Internet

After you get your feet wet with CompuServe, or if you're brave, before you join CompuServe, you've got to get on the *Net*. Sooner or later, you *will* be on it whether you want to or not, so you may as well take the plunge now and stay one step ahead of the sluggish masses. That way, when the rest of humanity is finally dragged kicking and screaming out to the final frontier, you will have already staked out your own corner of the Net. Swallow your pride, go buy yourself a pocket protector, and get thee to the Net! Here are some more reasons:

Internet e-mail

E-mail is still the most popular and widely available Internet service. You can use it to communicate with millions of people worldwide and subscribe to mailing lists of all kinds, and it looks really cool on your business card.

Usenet news groups

The number of news groups available has surpassed 10,000 at some providers. As the world's largest bulletin board, Usenet is the heart and soul of the Internet. Usually, each group maintains a FAQ (compilation of *frequently asked questions*), which is very helpful. Topics range from everything you can think of to some things you can't.

The Worldwide Web

You can use a Web browser program, such as NCSA Mosaic, to *surf* the Web. The Web is the ever-expanding, global collection of hypertext (interconnected/interconnectable documents) residing on the Internet. It's the fastest-growing part of the Net. The Web is full of multimedia and other fun stuff such as sounds, pictures, free programs (including Web browsers), and movies. You can put your personal or business "home page" on the Web for others to browse. Good browsers are capable of handling some e-mail functions, Usenet news groups, Gopher, file transfers, and hypertext.

Gopher

Gopher is an Internet service that reduces much of cyberspace to an endless series of easily navigated menus. You simply follow Gopher links that look interesting until you find the file or text or whatever strikes your fancy, and then you realize it's 2:00 in the morning. Using Gopher, you can find most everything on the Net.

File Transfer Protocol (FTP)

FTP sounds like the title of some techno-thriller, but all it means is that you can use it to send and retrieve files of all types all over the world from your desktop. If e-mail is like a superfast postal service, FTP is like a hyper FedEx or UPS.

You will become more valuable to current or future employers

It's true. In this era of downsizing, insecurity, and instability, the one shining example that appears to hold solid promise for the foreseeable future is the Internet. Being able to put your Internet skills on your resume dramatically enhances your value as a potential hire. If you're Internet-savvy, that makes you "forward-thinking," "cutting edge," "hi-tech," and any number of other buzzwords.

It's better for you than TV

As with the boob tube, in cyberspace you still slouch in front of a screen, but at least on the Net you get to actively partici-pate. Let's face it: The TV model features a zoned-out you, awash in programming and manipulated by unseen, faraway powers. The Internet model features you as an independent actor/explorer, using your imagination in an all-new digital landscape. Better to be a mouse potato than a couch potato.

You'll have something to talk about at the next cocktail party

Instead of staring mutely at the cheese dip, imagine boldly delivering reports from the digital frontier! What could make you more charming and mysterious than the ability to regale listeners with tales of electronic daredevilry? What topic perks up more ears than the Internet? Someone else at the party is bound to be on the Net, too, and before you know it, you're exchanging e-mail addresses and chatting about your favorite Web sites.

Impress everybody with your business card

If you're into impressing people, put your Internet address on your business cards right next to the number for your mobile phone, your car phone, your fax number, your home phone, and your home fax number.

To learn more about the Internet, pick up a copy of IDG's *The Internet For Dummies.*

Your Pipeline to the Internet

To get onto the Internet, you need to subscribe to an Internet provider. The Pipeline is one provider that offers very powerful and easy-to-use software, and the software's free. The point-and-click program organizes the fast and loose Net into logical topic groups and integrates its features, including the Web, seamlessly.

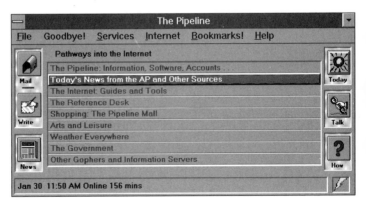

It provides full access to everything the Internet has to offer: Universal electronic mail, 10,000+ discussion groups, and a cornucopia of resources ranging from on-line books to instant storm forecasts, from today's Supreme Court opinions to live, real-time conversations with people anywhere in the world. **The Pipeline.** 150 Broadway, Suite 610, New York, NY 10038. For information about subscriptions and software, you can reach The Pipeline at 212-267-3636 (voice), 212-267-4380 (fax), or 212-267-8606 (modem — up to 28.8kbps, V.34 — log-in as a guest). To request information about The Pipeline by e-mail, address your e-mail message to info@pipeline.com. Internet users can also "gopher" directly to pipeline.com or "ftp" directly to ftp.pipeline.com.

E-Mail Messaging

In the preceding two sections, I've briefly explained the benefits of going on-line. Now I want to offer some tips about the ins and outs of e-mail.

E-mail is an electronic medium that millions of people use to share information. It's become extremely popular in corporate America because it's more efficient than using the telephone, less formal than writing a letter, and much faster than snail mail (the United States Postal Service). When e-mail is used properly, it's a huge time-saver because it allows you to share information with someone down the hall, or halfway across the world, in just a moment's time. But if you're spending one, two, or even three hours per day responding to your e-mail messages, it can become an enormous time waster because it takes away from the time that you should be spending on your other work.

Keep it short and sweet

The whole concept behind using e-mail is that it's fast, short, and sweet. You don't worry about spelling, punctuation, or grammatical errors. You don't edit or proofread your writing. You just write your message and send it. It's sort of like an electronic memo pad.

Make it easy to read

Even though most e-mail messages are less than three paragraphs in length, you should put your most important information in the first sentence of the first paragraph and your background or supporting information in the following paragraphs.

Use the subject line

The subject line is the most important part of your e-mail message. It's the first thing the recipient sees, so it should be short, concise, descriptive, and informative. If action is required on the part of the reader, put it in the subject line — for example, "Please attend Tues. meeting" or "Need Reply by Wed. morning."

Make your subject line so descriptive that it grabs your readers' attention and will make them want to read your message first. You often have 25 to 35 characters for a subject line, so make the most of them.

Keep the message simple

When you write your e-mail message, write short, easy-to-read sentences and paragraphs. As mentioned earlier, put the most important information in the first few sentences of the first paragraph. Here are some tips:

- Try to keep your e-mail messages on one screen. If a message takes more than one screen, you should shorten it.

- If you're including a list of items, use a bulleted or numbered list. It's easier to read (like this list).

- If you must send a long message, attach the file as an enclosure. Write a brief description of the message in the subject line. The e-mail message itself should be a more detailed description of the enclosed file.

- When you attach a document to an e-mail message, write a brief but thorough description about the document you're sending. Don't forget to include the purpose of the document, detailed instructions regarding what the recipient is supposed to do with the document, and the date you need a response. This item of business should then be added to your Master List or into ACT!.

If you receive an e-mail message that's stamped with a receipt notification and you don't want to open it, just forward a *copy* of the message to yourself and read the copy.

Write e-mail messages that are easy to respond to

Make it easy for people to respond to your e-mail messages. When you write your message, be sure to include enough information so that recipients can give you a quick answer or response. Phrase your messages so that readers can reply with a "Yes" or "No," and if you're going to ask for a reply, mention it in your subject line.

E-mail etiquette

There are all sorts of *informal* rules, regulations, and other requirements for writing proper e-mail messages. Here are some of them.

- Don't send carbon copies (Cc) of messages to people who don't *have* to see the message.

- Don't send out blind copies (Bcc) casually; they can imply that you're going behind someone's back.

- Don't ask for a receipt unless it's *really* necessary. If you do, you may be insulting the recipients because you're implying that they don't read their mail.

- Beware of crying wolf too many times. Use the "urgent message" notation sparingly. If you use it too often, your future messages may be ignored.

- Don't use all capital letters! WHEN YOU TYPE YOUR MESSAGE IN ALL CAPITALS, IT'S KNOWN AS *SHOUTING* IN THE E-MAIL WORLD. And I shouldn't have to remind you that people don't like to be shouted at. Use upper- and lowercase letters just as you would when you type an old-fashioned letter.

- Put addresses in the To, Copies (Cc), and Blind Copies (Bcc) lines in alphabetical order by the recipients' last names. Doing so keeps you from accidentally insulting people — such as your boss, supervisor, or manager — because you listed them in the wrong place. (If you're going to go out of your way to insult someone, do it on purpose!)

- Don't overuse your mailing list. Only send your messages to people who *need* to receive your message. By limiting your list of recipients, you'll build your credibility as an e-mail sender. The fewer messages you send, the greater the attention they receive.

- Send only those messages that are work related. Messages such as jokes or invitations to nonwork-related events are best handled outside of e-mail.

- Type positive messages so that your readers will look forward to reading them. Even when you must communicate a negative message, try your best to say it in a positive way.

- If your message is very important, controversial, confidential, or could easily be misunderstood, use the telephone or set up a face-to-face meeting.

But I get too much e-mail

If you're getting too much e-mail or it's taking too many hours of your day to respond to all of it, maybe somebody isn't using the e-mail system in the manner in which it was intended. So let me ask you a question: How much time would you spend reading and responding to these messages if they had been sent to you the old fashioned way, on paper?

Would you be in such a hurry to respond to them and get them off your desk? Would you drop everything and deal with them immediately? Of course not! In the old days, these paper memos could sit in your in-box for days, if not weeks, before you got around to them, and the world didn't come to an end.

But because the same message is now being sent to you electronically, you feel this primal urge to read and respond to it immediately. But are you in such a hurry to read your e-mail messages because they're so very important or because you know that if you don't get to them regularly, they will just back up on you and eventually overwhelm you? Here are some tips on how to cope with the e-mail onslaught:

- Set aside specific times during the day that you'll go through your e-mail to see what's arrived and what's important. Don't interrupt yourself every time an e-mail message arrives.

- If it's not necessary for you to respond to each and every e-mail message that you receive, don't!

- When you must respond to an e-mail message, make your response short and sweet. Give "Yes" and "No" answers when possible, and if you have to write a few sentences or paragraphs, make them concise and to the point.

- If you're getting copied (Cc) or blind copied (Bcc) e-mail messages that don't specifically apply to your job or daily responsibilities, ask the people who have been sending these messages to take you off their lists.

- Don't allow the arrival of e-mail to interrupt your important work. If your computer beeps or sounds a trumpet to announce the arrival of each new e-mail message, turn this feature off. And if your computer's hard drive starts making all sorts of whirring noises whenever you get an e-mail message, you may want to turn off your e-mail as well.

Check your e-mail box regularly. If you don't check your e-mail box regularly, you lose the major advantage of using e-mail over snail mail.

Be careful with the freedom of e-mail

Just because e-mail's supposed to be an unstructured environment, you shouldn't allow yourself to get carried away. There's just too big a difference between writing e-mail messages to your boss, colleagues, and coworkers, and writing anonymous messages on the Internet. When writing e-mail messages to the people within your own company or organization, you should use the same diction and common sense that you would use if you were writing a letter, having a conversation on the phone, or having a face-to-face meeting.

Don't flame out

If you're feeling hurt, angry, or insulted about something, don't write out your thoughts as an e-mail message and send it off, especially if you're upset with your boss, manager, or supervisor. In e-mail lingo, the term for this use of e-mail is called *flaming*.

When people let their emotions flare up and then send blistering e-mail messages, they're flaming. (It's sort of like throwing a temper tantrum.) And when the person who receives the message fires off a fiery response, you've got yourself a *flame war*. (We used to have these kinds of fights — food fights — in the high school cafeteria. But this is the 90s, and we're more civilized now.)

Try your best not to become a participant in a flame war, especially at the office. You've certainly got more important things to do. In most instances, the sender just sent a message that you misinterpreted, or vice versa. Or maybe the sender wrote something stupid, or vice versa. If you have a problem with someone, pick up the phone or schedule a face-to-face meeting so that you can talk things out.

Protect yourself against e-mail break-ins

If you leave your computer unattended, make sure that no one else can use your e-mail program while you're away. You certainly don't want someone else writing a letter to *your* boss describing what *you* think of him or her. And never give your e-mail user name and password to anyone else.

Save important information

When you send or receive an e-mail message that contains important information, print out a copy of it and put it in the appropriate file so that you can find it when you need it.

Smileys improve e-mail communication :-)

Because e-mail messages can easily be misunderstood or misinterpreted, e-mail junkies often use smileys to convey feelings, moods, or emotions.

To see a smiley, you must put your left ear to your left shoulder and look at the computer screen sideways. Today, there are hundreds of smileys. Here's a sampling of some smileys and their meanings:

Smiley	Meaning
:-)	Happy
:-(	Sad
:-I I	Angry
%-)	Happy confused
8-O	Shocked
;-)	Winking
:'-(	Crying
:-*	Kiss
X-(	Brain dead

Part VI
Planning Your Out-of-Town Travel

Packing Your Luggage

The three words "I forgot something" strike terror in the hearts of all travelers. On the following pages, you'll learn how to do a more thorough job of planning and preparing for your business and personal trips.

Make a list of everything you need to do in preparation for your trip. This list would include things you need to purchase, people you need to call, and anything else that comes to mind. As you complete each item, check it off the list.

Lay everything you *think* you'll absolutely, positively need to take with you on your bed before you start packing. Then go through each item, one by one, and put the stuff you *really* don't need back in the closet or dresser drawer.

When you're traveling in the U.S., you can probably replace anything you forget to bring with you with an acceptable substitute. However, when you're traveling outside the U.S., you *must* always bring everything with you that you'll need. Even the simplest things, the things that we take for granted, are often hard, if not impossible, to get in foreign countries.

Things to pack

- Enough underwear and socks to last the trip — one pair per day.

- Enough outerwear to last the trip.

- Essential toiletries.

- A battery-powered clock and/or clock radio.

- A steamer and/or a travel iron with fold-down handles.

- A folding hair dryer and a curling iron. (Remember to bring along a voltage converter and plugs if you're traveling outside the U.S..)

- For men: a travel electric shaver with built-in 110/220 volt converters.

- A portable radio or Walkman.

- An emergency medical kit that contains your favorite painkiller, a cold remedy, an upset-stomach medicine, and Band-Aids.

- An umbrella.

When traveling overseas, bring a 220 volt power converter and plug adapters.

If you don't want to bring a traveling iron, you can usually borrow an iron and ironing board from the hotel.

A Swiss army knife has lots of features that can come in handy while you're traveling.

If you can't live without coffee in the morning, bring along a small coffee kit — including little packets of instant coffee, sugar, and powdered cream — with an immersion heater.

Packing toiletries: smaller is better

Here are some tips on packing toiletries:

- Take the smallest possible size of each of your toiletries. If small sizes aren't available, buy some small containers and take only as much as you need.

- To make sure that your bottles don't leak and stain your clothes, place them in a plastic baggy.

- For women: Keep duplicates of all your cosmetics so you can leave them packed at all times.

- Keep a duplicate toiletries travel bag with your razor, shaving cream, (or electric razor), toothbrush, tooth paste, nail clippers, deodorant, lotion, and so on.

Zip-lock plastic bags are great for holding small miscellaneous things as well as wet bathing suits and leaky bottles.

Choosing Clothing

- Bring along enough underwear, socks, and nylons for the whole trip.

- Pack clothes that are neutral in color and don't show wrinkles or dirt.

- Take clothes that mix and match.

- Bring two pairs of shoes. Wear one; pack one.

- Bring comfortable clothing to wear in your hotel room.

- If you're bringing two suits (outfits), wear one and pack one.

- Wear clothes that are made of wrinkle-resistant fibers.

Tips for women

- As you're laying your outfits on the bed, try to think of everything that goes with each particular outfit: shoes, belt, stockings, slip, necklace, earrings, and so forth.

- To make your outfits look different, bring along a few extra scarves and/or blouses.

- In addition to packing enough underwear, bring some extra pairs of socks and extra pantyhose that *fit.*

- For casual wear, leggings are great. They're comfortable and they don't take up much space. (Don't bring jeans because they're bulky.)

- Pack a comfortable pair of slippers.

- Wear or pack a pair of business shoes — black works with everything — and plan your wardrobe so that everything works together.

- Bring/wear a second pair of comfortable shoes. Make sure that both pairs have low to medium heels (up to $1^1/_2$ inches). You want your feet to be comfortable.

- Carry a light trench coat on the airplane.

Never pack your jewelry. Only bring a few pieces that will go with everything.

Tips for men

- Bring/wear one pair of dress shoes (black) and a comfortable pair of running shoes.

- Pack casual clothes, like sweats, for lounging in your room.

- Pack one suit and wear the other (if your trip is long enough to require two suits).

When you arrive in your hotel room, hang your suits up as soon as possible. You can steam out wrinkles by hanging your suits in the bathroom and turning on the shower and running hot water for 10 to 15 minutes.

If you don't feel like packing several suits, shirts, socks, underwear, T-shirts, and other clothing, have the hotel's dry cleaning or laundry service wash them for you. (Make sure that your company will reimburse you for this expense because it's not cheap.)

If you're meeting new or different people every day, they won't know that you've only got two ties with you.

Choosing Carry-On Items

If you'll be checking your luggage, here's a list of items that you should consider carrying with you on the plane:

- Your valuables: your cash, credit cards, traveler's checks, and your jewelry.

- Your airline tickets, passport, visas, and tour vouchers.

- Your prescription medicine, over-the-counter drugs, house and car keys, and eyeglasses.

- Any important business or personal papers and anything that has sentimental value.

- Any fragile or breakable items, such as your camera, eyeglasses, contact lens (with case and solution), hearing aid with extra batteries, and any glass containers.

- Name, address, and phone number of destination hotel, business contacts, and/or relatives at destination.

- Clothing for your first day at the destination, should you have something important to do that day.

- Always bring some toiletries and one change of underwear if you're checking your luggage. (If the airline misplaces your luggage, it may be a few days before they find it and return it to you.)

- Toothbrush and toothpaste in a zip-lock plastic bag.

- Breath mints.

- Comb and brush.

- Makeup, hair spray, styling mousse, spare earrings.

- For men, a shaving kit.

Pack your jewelry, prescription medicine, and other valuable things in a small bag and place it at the top of your carry-on bag. If, for some reason, you're required to check your carry-on bag, it's easy for you to remove your valuables and keep them on your person.

 Don't pack anything in a carry-on bag that could be considered a weapon (scissors, a knife, and so on).

If you're hungry, bring your own food and something to drink. It's always a good idea to bring bottled water because it's very easy to become dehydrated.

 Clean out your purse or wallet and leave the stuff you don't need at home. This could include your library card, the local grocery store's check cashing card, and the health club's photo-ID.

Before you leave the house or your office, *check to see that you have your tickets!* Look in your briefcase, purse, travel bag, or coat pocket several times before you walk out the door and one final time before your car, taxi, or limo drives away.

Here are some additional travel tips:

- Use a luggage cart. It makes carrying your luggage much easier.

- Instead of carrying a briefcase, bring a large tote that can double as your briefcase.

- Bring along an inflatable neck pillow. An inflatable neck pillow cushions your neck and holds your head up while you doze off on the plane.

- If you tend to perspire, you might want to pack a fresh shirt or blouse and some anti-perspirant.

- Purchase carry-on bags that have large, outside-zippered compartments. You can use them to store your in-flight reading material. Put your luggage in the overhead bin with the zippered compartment on top. This way, it's easy to retrieve a magazine, book, or some of your business materials.

- Use a small travel case to store all of the things that you would like to keep with you during your flight. Keep the travel case in the outside zippered compartment of your carry-on bag. Then once you're aboard the plane, remove the case from your carry-on bag just before you place it in the overhead compartment.

- If you wear contact lenses, remove them during the flight and wear your glasses instead.

- Just before landing, take your toiletry bag with you to the washroom and freshen up.

- When you're flying in casual clothes and have an important business or social meeting planned upon your arrival or for the next day, *always* carry your clothing with you.

 You can also store your magazines, books, and business materials in your briefcase or a small carry-on bag that fits under the seat.

 I know I'm repeating myself, but when you leave your home or office for the airport, always check to see that you've got your airline ticket and your passport if you are leaving the country. (I always check one final time when I get into the car, taxi, or limo.)

Packing Your Luggage

- Don't overpack checked bags. This puts pressure on the latches, making it easier for them to spring open. A heavy bag that fits in an overhead bin may still cause the bin to exceed its weight limit.

- Lock your bags. Locks aren't very effective against determined thieves, but they make it harder for the bags to spring open accidentally.

- Put a bright, colorful luggage tag on the outside of your baggage. It should include your name, home address, and home and work phone numbers. Such tags will make it easy for you to spot your bags as they come down the carousel.

- Put your name, address, and phone number information *inside* each bag and add an address and telephone number where you can be reached at your destination city.

 Always bring something to keep you occupied: one or two good books (preferably paperback), some magazines, and a Walkman radio, CD player, or cassette player. (If you bring a Game Boy, remember to turn off the sound.)

Don't forget to bring all of the papers and other support material you need for your business trips.

Bring expense reports, a letter-sized pad of paper, pens and pencils, a pocket tape recorder, and your detailed itinerary (including names, addresses, phone numbers, and the dates and times of your meetings). Also include a list of hotels, car rental agencies, and a list of important phone numbers for people you may have to contact while you're out of town.

Leave a copy of your itinerary with your secretary, assistant, or manager; a family member or neighbor; and the people you'll be meeting with while you're out of town.

Ticket, passport, cash, and credit cards are all things you can't afford to misplace.

Checking In at the Airport

Here are some tips for checking in at the airport:

- Don't check in at the last minute. Even if you make the flight, your bag may not.

- Watch the agent who is checking your bags to make sure that he or she attaches a destination tag to each one. Then check to see that these tags show the three-letter code for your destination airport.

- Ask where your bags are being checked to. (They may not be checked to your final destination if you must clear customs before you reach your final destination or if you're taking a connecting flight involving two airlines that don't have an interline baggage agreement.)

- Always get a claim check for every bag that you check. Don't throw the claim checks away until your bags are returned and you have left the baggage-claim area.

- Always remove any airline tags that might still be on the bag from your last trip.

If the value of the contents of your baggage is worth more than the airline's liability limit (usually $1250 per passenger for domestic flights and $640 per bag on international trips), consider purchasing excess valuation insurance from the airline.

TIP If you need any type of assistance — you've got a sore leg or sore back and don't feel like walking to the gate — ask one of the airline employees if it's possible to have someone drive you to your gate in the golf cart.

Getting Your Bags after Your Flight

- Make sure that you have the right bag since so many bags look alike. Always check the bag tags.

- If your bag arrives open, unlocked, or visibly damaged, check immediately to see if any of the contents are missing or damaged.

- Report any baggage problems to your airline before leaving the airport.

- If the airline loses your bags, insist that the airline fill out a form and give you a copy, even if they say the bags will be in on the next flight. Get the agent's name and an appropriate telephone number for following up (not the reservations number).

- If the airline takes your baggage claim checks, make sure this is noted on all copies of the claim report.

- If the airline misplaces your luggage, ask the airline before you leave the airport if it will deliver the bags when they're found without charge to your home or hotel. Also, ask if the airline will give you an advance or reimburse you for any items you must buy while your bag is missing.

- If your luggage is lost on a U.S. domestic trip (a trip starting and ending within the U.S. and not a connection to an international flight) the airline may owe you $1250 or more. To be reimbursed, you need to notify the airline of the loss, delay, or damage to your luggage *in writing* within seven days of the time when you should have received the luggage. You will also need to provide receipts of your expenses. (Send your letter to the head of the airline's local office in the city where the luggage was lost. Send a copy of your letter to the airline's corporate office.)

- If your luggage was lost on an international trip, the airline's liability for loss, delay or damage is approximately nine dollars per pound. (Since the average bag weighs less than 44 pounds, you may receive almost $400. You may be able to get more if you told the agent that your luggage was more valuable at the time you checked in, assuming that your luggage never shows up.

When you're talking with the baggage clerks or other airline personnel, try to give them an accurate description of your luggage; it may make it easier for them to find it.

Write a *nice* letter. When you write your letter to the customer relations office, include your frequent flyer number, if you have one, and go into great detail about how terribly you were inconvenienced by the loss of your luggage as you ask for compensation. You should include an itemized list of the replacement items you needed to purchase.

When you get to your hotel, always open your suitcase immediately. If something is missing or has been damaged, call the airline immediately. Make a note of the name and position or title of the person you spoke to, as well as the date and time of the call. Ask the person what you should do next and confirm this conversation with a certified letter.

Making the Most of Your Waiting Time

Traveling today is a real pain in the butt. I don't care what the airlines say; all we ever do is sit and wait, and wait, and wait. We wait to board the plane. We wait for it to leave the gate. We wait for the plane to take off. We wait for it to land. And if we don't carry everything we own on board, we wait for our luggage. The following travel tips should help to reduce the stress and strain of airplane travel:

- When you're traveling, expect to encounter delays in your air travel plans. Planes are always delayed because of mechanical problems, the weather, or lots of other things that the airlines never tell us about. So prepare for those delays by bringing additional work that you can do on the plane and a list of people to call if you're stuck in the airport. And in case you need to take a break, bring along some magazines, a good book, and your Walkman with your favorite audio cassette.

- Traffic to the airport is always troublesome, especially when you're running late, so always leave yourself some extra commuting time. If you're driving — as opposed to taking public transportation, a taxi, or limo — and are unfamiliar with the local roads, allow yourself a bit more time because you could get lost.

- If you're going to leave your car in an airport parking lot, allow extra time to find a parking spot, (most of the airports are short of parking). Public transportation, a taxi, or a limo may be an attractive alternative. If you frequently use the same car rental company, you may be able to leave your car in the rental company's parking lot and take the courtesy van to and from the terminal.

- Once you get inside the terminal, anticipate delays at security checkpoints and passenger check-ins. Infrequent fliers always hold up the line.

- Always arrive at your gate at least 20 minutes before the scheduled departure. If you don't, the airline can bump you and give your seat to someone else without providing any compensation. (Airlines commonly overbook their available seats.)

- When selecting a seat, don't sit in a first row (bulkhead) seat. Parents traveling with infants are usually seated there. An exit row may be a better option and usually offers more leg room.

- Always be one of the first people to board the plane. This will guarantee that you'll be able to store your carry-on luggage in one of the overhead bins. Then you can settle in your seat and start working while the latecomers are trying to find a place to put their bags.

- If you're hungry, bring your own food and beverage. Most airlines are cutting back on their in-flight meals (which aren't very good in the first place) and are only offering peanuts and soft drinks. (If you want to have some fun with the flight attendants, stop at a deli on your way to the airport and pick up a nice fat sandwich; it makes them go crazy.)

- If you need to confirm the time of an arriving or departing flight, call your airline's automated flight arrival and departure lines for estimated times instead of waiting for a reservations agent.

- If you know you're going to need a rental car, always call in advance and make a reservation. If you're going to be arriving late, call the car rental company, from the airplane if necessary, to let them know that you're still coming.

TIP

If you're tired of listening to annoying and distracting noises while you're flying, try Noise Cancellation Technologies's NoiseBuster. NoiseBuster's "anti-noisewave" technology blocks out the constant drone of the airplane's engines and lots of other unwanted sounds — like screaming children — and allows you to concentrate on your work and hear yourself think. I use NoiseBuster whenever I fly and find that I actually feel relaxed and refreshed after my flight. **NoiseBuster.** Noise Cancellation Technologies, Inc., 800 Summer Street, Stanford, CT 06901, 800-278-3526.

Selecting Your Flights

Here are some thoughts on making your airline travel easier:

- Take the earliest flight available. An early departure is less likely to be delayed because of the ripple effects of delays throughout the day.

- Fly Tuesdays through Thursdays or Sunday mornings.

- Try not to go to the airport at the busy times — the times when everybody else is going to the airport.

- Get a good travel agent and train him or her to get you seat assignments you want.

- Always get your seat assignments, with boarding passes, for the entire trip.

- Avoid bulkhead seats. There's no seat in front of you under which to place small items you may need in flight, and young children are often placed in the bulkhead rows.

- Always have alternate plans in case of flight delays or cancellations.

Purchasing Your Ticket

- Purchase your ticket with a credit card. This payment method may provide you with certain protections under federal credit regulations, which can be meaningful should the airline declare bankruptcy.

- When you receive your ticket, check to make sure that all of the information on it is correct.

- Fares change all the time, so check frequently to see if the cost of your ticket has gone down. If it has, you can have your ticket reissued at the lower fare.

- Always try to have your tickets and boarding passes in hand before you go to the airport. This speeds your check-in process.

- Always reconfirm your flight a day or two before your scheduled departure because flight schedules do change.

The check-in

- Check in at least 30 minutes before your flight. Airlines can give your reserved seat to someone else even if you already have your boarding pass. (You can lose your entire reservation if you haven't checked in 10 minutes before scheduled departure time on a domestic flight. If a flight is oversold, the last passengers to check in are the first to be bumped, even if they have met the 10-minute deadline.)

- Bring a photo ID with your name on it when you fly. (Many airlines are requesting such identification at check-in to reduce the reselling of discount tickets.)

- After you check in, examine your ticket to make sure that the agent didn't accidentally remove two coupons.

Be nice, polite, and patient with the airline ticket agent who is checking you in, and be nice to the people who drive the golf carts. They're the people who can help you if you've got a problem.

If you're bumped

- If you are bumped because your flight is overbooked, read the Overbooking Notice in your ticket and then ask for a copy of the rules mentioned in that notice. (This information only applies to oversold flights.)

- If the airline offers you a free ticket, ask about restrictions. How long is the ticket good for? Is it blacked out during holiday periods when you might want to use it? Can it be used for international flights? Most importantly, can you make a reservation, and if so, how far before departure are you permitted to make it?

Planning Your Business Trip

When you're planning your trip, write out an itinerary. You should include the names, addresses, and phone and fax numbers of everybody you'll be meeting and the hotels where you'll be staying. It should also include the beginning and ending times for your meetings.

Send a copy of your itinerary to each one of the people that you'll be meeting with.

Before you leave, always call ahead to confirm your meeting plans. You don't want to fly across the country to learn that the person you're supposed to be meeting with is out of the country.

When you meet people, take their business cards and read them to yourself several times so you that can remember their names.

Making Your Hotel Reservation

When you make your hotel reservation, here are some of the questions that you should think about:

- What is the hotel's room availability, and how many rooms do you need?

- Do you want a smoking or non-smoking room?

- What size, type, or kind of bed do you want?
- What is the price? What does it include? Taxes and service? Breakfast? Do they offer discounts?
- Does the view change the price? Garden view? Water view?
- What form of payment do they accept?
- What form of payment do they accept for a deposit?
- What is their cancellation policy?
- If you're driving, do they have a parking facility? If so, is there a charge?

When you've finished your conversation, take down the hotel's confirmation number and ask them to send you a written confirmation.

 Always ask for directions from the airport/train station to the hotel. If you'll be taking a taxi, ask what the estimated cost should be.

 Always confirm your reservations a few days before you're scheduled to arrive.

Staying Safe in Your Hotel Room

Hotels with good security never give out guest room numbers or other guest information. And the reservations clerk never announces a guest's room number or places a guest's room key room number side up when other people are in a position to see it.

Here are some tips to keep you safe and sound while you're in your hotel room:

- Never open your hotel room door without looking through the peephole first. If you don't know the person, or if the person claims to be with the hotel staff and you know you didn't send for anyone, call the front desk or hotel security to verify whether or not this uninvited visitor is who he or she claims to be.

- Never invite strangers you just met to come to your room.

- If the room door has a key-type lock, insist that the cylinder be changed before accepting the room. (For additional security, you can purchase a personal alarm that fits inside the door jam of your room.)

- Always keep a good hold on your room key and make sure that, upon opening your room door, you remember to remove the key. Do not leave it dangling in your lock. If you are afraid that you may lose it while out, leave it with the desk clerk for safe keeping.

- Rooms located near an exit can provide easy access for criminals.

- Never leave exit/fire doors propped open. The doors are there to keep you safe.

- Never remove or disconnect the battery from your smoke detector.

- Don't leave your laptop or notebook computer lying around in your hotel room. Lock it in your suitcase. (You can purchase small, programmable, motion detector alarms to protect your computer.)

- Small children should *always* be accompanied by an adult at the hotel swimming pool, even if a hotel life guard is present.

- Never use your hotel room for business! Always conduct any business meeting in the hotel lobby, the restaurant, or the lounge.

Keeping in Touch with the Folks Back Home

When you take a trip, designate one person at home as your contact person. This is the person you'll call for any messages. And tell all your family and friends that if they must get in touch with you, they should leave a message with that one person. The frequency of your calls will depend upon the nature — and length — of your personal or business travel.

Your contact person should have a copy of your schedule and itinerary, complete with hotel names, phone numbers, and fax numbers if possible. The fax is a convenient way to communicate with you when you're many time zones away from home.

 Make sure that someone knows how to get in touch with you at all times. (This may be even more important when you're traveling for fun rather than business.)

 Don't use the hotel phone! It's the most expensive way to make a call because hotels routinely add stiff surcharges to long-distance phone calls. Use a telephone credit card instead.

 If you're traveling abroad, AT&T's USA Direct is a great service. You dial a local access number in your host country and are connected with an AT&T operator who then connects your call in the U.S.. The call is charged to your AT&T Calling Card or as a collect call to your home or business telephone. AT&T has a companion service, AT&T World Connect, which allows you to call a person in country B while you are in country A. For additional information, call your AT&T representative or 800-331-1140.

Traveling with Your Computer

Computers are great, and you can do some amazing things with those three- or four-pound notebooks. But they aren't much good if they run out of juice or you can't connect them to the hotel's telephone. So when you're traveling with a computer, think about your communication needs *before* you leave for the airport. Here are some tips:

- When you make your hotel reservation, request a modem-ready room. (Most of the major hotel chains have installed modem-ready telephones.)

- Make sure that your laptop is fully charged when you arrive at the airport. Security personnel might ask you to turn it on to verify that it's a real computer.

- Always bring along a fully charged replacement battery so that you can continue working after the first one runs out of energy.

- If you're carrying a brand new, super-duper, fancy-schmancy computer, don't flaunt it. Store it in a plain but sturdy briefcase or traveling bag so that it won't be a tempting target for thieves.

- Bring along a collection of extension cords so that you can use your portable computer comfortably in your hotel room. Include an extension power cord, an extension phone line cord, and extra in-line and duplex phone jacks. (When you check out in the morning, don't forget to pack everything up and take it with you.)

- Always travel with a screwdriver and a pocket knife so that you can remove wall plates and strip insulation from phone wires, if necessary. If you really want to be prepared, bring along an acoustic coupler to attach to your phone, alligator clips to attach your modem to phone wires, and a line tester to locate live phone wires.

- When traveling overseas, check your computer's power adapter. Make sure it can accommodate 110/120 and 220/240 voltages and line frequencies of 50/60Hz. Don't forget to bring along power adapter plugs that fit the electrical outlets of the countries you'll be visiting. An assortment of electrical wall plugs can be found at most computer stores.

- Bring along some blank disks to back up your information and a bootable floppy disk if you can't get your computer to start.

Password protect your information

Always protect your information with a password. You should use your computer's password protection so that someone else can't even turn it on (in addition to putting a password on each of your applications).

When selecting a password, don't choose one that's easy to figure out — like the name of your wife or your daughter. On the other hand, you don't want to select a password that's so hard to remember that you have to write it down.

Expense reporting made easy

One thing that everybody hates to do when they're traveling is complete their expense reports, and QuickXpense from Portable Software makes this dreadful, boring, and time-consuming task much easier. You enter your expenses in the same way you enter items in your checkbook register.

The more you use the program, the easier it gets because QuickXpense remembers all of your expense information, such as account numbers, airlines, hotels, and restaurants. It even remembers the people you've had meetings with and can link this information with ACT!, WinFax Pro, and other programs. When you're finished entering your expenses, QuickXpense will organize it for you. All you have to do is print the form. **QuickXpense.** QuickXpense, Portable Software Corporation, 11400 SE 8th Street, Bellevue, WA 98004, 800-626-8620.

Using CompuServe to Stay in Touch

When you're traveling, you can use CompuServe in just the same way you use it when you're at home or in the office. Here are a few tips on how CompuServe can help you when you're out of town:

- If you're in your hotel room and need to print a document, just use CompuServe. If you have faxing software, you can send yourself a fax to the hotel's fax machine. And if you don't, you can send yourself an e-mail message, but instead of sending it as e-mail, send it as a fax to the hotel's fax machine. Then go down to the front desk to pick it up.

- If you need to send a fax back to your office or to someone else, once again you can use CompuServe instead of the hotel's faxing services. It's much cheaper and will not include any of the hotel's long-distance phone charges.

- And if you've run out of things to do in your hotel room, log onto your favorite CompuServe forum and have a nice on-line conversation with your CompuPals. (When you're in the towns of your on-line friends, why not invite them to meet you for a cup of coffee?)

If you do a lot of traveling — both domestic and international — and you're not already a member of CompuServe, you should consider joining. CompuServe is the most international of all the major on-line services and can be reached by a local call in more than 700 cities around the world. **CompuServe.** 5000 Arlington Centre Blvd., Columbus, OH 43220, 800-848-8990. (If you're already a CompuServe member, you can get a list of all of the local access numbers for thousands of locations in the United States, Canada, and other countries around the world by typing GO PHONES.)

A friend told me that when he was vacationing in Australia, he used CompuServe to send his daughter a fax. (She is not a CompuServe member, so he couldn't send her e-mail.) The cost of sending the fax from Australia to the United States was under $1.

Use WinFax Pro to Send and Receive Your Faxes

With WinFax Pro you can send and receive all your faxes directly from your computer, without ever touching a piece of paper.

Sending a fax is as easy as printing a letter

Sending a fax from within a Windows application — like your word processor — is as easy as printing a letter. When you're ready to send your fax, select WinFax Pro as your printer and click the print button. Look through your fax phone book, select the person to whom you wish to send the fax, add a cover page, press the send button, and it's done. This is indeed a great time-saver when you're on the road.

ACT! integrates seamlessly with WinFax Pro. Just click on the WinFax Pro icon (from within ACT!'s word processor), and the document will be sent as a fax within a few moments.

You get to keep working

WinFax Pro runs in the background. So while you're working on a document, spreadsheet, or your expense reports, your fax is being transmitted.

Forward copies of your faxes

Would you like to send a copy of one of your faxes — or a copy of a fax that you just received — to someone else while you're in your hotel room? If so, the process is very simple. You select the file you wish to fax, select the person to whom you wish to fax it, add a cover sheet, and press the send button.

Group your documents together

Do you often need to send a person several different documents that were created in different software programs (for example, a letter from your word processor, tables from one of your spreadsheets, and illustrations from your drawing package)? If so, in WinFax Pro, you can group them together and send them in the same fax transmission.

Sending scanned documents

You can scan a document, newspaper article, photograph, or anything else, and fax the scanned image directly from your computer. (Though you probably won't have a scanner with you while you're traveling.)

Place your corporate logo, letterhead, or signature on your faxes

It's easy to place your corporate logo, business letterhead, or signature on your faxed letters and correspondence. Just fax or scan your logo, letterhead, or signature into your computer, where it is saved as a graphic image. Then insert the image in the appropriate place within your document.

The phone book

Another great timesaving feature of WinFax Pro is the phone book. When you're traveling, you've got a directory of the names and voice and fax numbers of everybody you send faxes to. Note that ACT! and WinFax Pro can share each other's phone books.

To send the same fax to several people, just create a group in your phone book, and WinFax Pro will send the fax to everybody in the group. This method is a whole lot easier than sending it to each person, one fax at a time.

Receiving faxes

One of the beautiful features of WinFax Pro is that you can receive faxes directly into your computer.

The Fax MailBox

WinFax Pro has a unique service that allows you to receive a fax from your own fax mailbox. Delrina's Fax MailBox is an enhanced fax messaging service that offers you your own fax mailbox with your own 800 number. The Fax MailBox receives and stores faxes until you decide to retrieve them. You can retrieve your faxes at any time, directly into WinFax Pro, or by simply dialing into your mailbox by phone and forwarding all your faxes to any fax machine. This is a great way to guarantee that you'll always get your faxes when you're on the road.

Annotating your faxes

While you're reading your fax, you can write electronic notes to yourself in the margins or circle and highlight other parts of the fax that you think are important. When you've finished, the fax, with your notations, can once again be saved, printed, or sent on to someone else.

Converting your faxes to editable (not edible) text

One of the great features of WinFax Pro is its capability to convert a faxed or scanned image into basic computer text that can be edited in your word processor. (The process of converting a faxed or scanned image into text is called *optical character recognition,* abbreviated *OCR.*) With OCR, you eliminate the tedious and time-consuming job of retyping your faxes so that you can use the information in another document. This feature is a big time-saver, especially when you're on the road, because you can take the information from the fax that you just received and put it into a document or letter without having to retype any of the information.

And if you're in your hotel room and need to print a document, just send a fax to the hotel's fax machine. Then go down to the front desk to pick it up.

(**WinFax Pro.** WinFax Pro, Delrina Technology Inc., 6830 Via Del Oro, San Jose, CA 95119, 800-268-6082.)

Protecting Yourself While You're Traveling

While you're traveling, you should always be alert and aware of everything that's going on around you.

Be wary when you're traveling

You are most theft prone while visiting tourist attractions.

- Be very suspicious of anyone who comes up to you and remarks about something on your clothes, or who asks you a question with the intention of distracting you. Frequently, this person is part of a team. While he or she has your attention, the teammate has your wallet.

- If using public transportation, be especially alert to those around you who might try to jostle you.

- Watch out for motorbikes coming up from behind. Keep your purse, if you have one, away from the street side and hang onto it as the motorbike passes. Don't let it swing loosely from your shoulder.

- Wear an internal money pouch around your neck and under your clothes if possible.

- Don't keep your wallet in your back hip pocket. You have no idea how easily a deft pickpocket can lift it out!

- Never leave anything, not even an umbrella, visible inside your rental car. You increase your chances of being robbed by 60 percent.

- Never leave your car unattended — or where you can't see it — when it's packed with your belongings.

Don't make yourself an easy target

You don't want to make yourself an *easy* target, so always be wary of:

- Small groups of loiterers in parking lots, alleyways, and doorways.

- Individuals who are watching you go into a bank or ATM area.

- People who are sitting in parked cars and appear to be watching you.

- Loiterers in public places.

- People who are following you from place to place.

- People who are near you in confined areas, such as between parked cars, in passageways, subways, or garages.

- Strangers who ask you for the time or other information. They may be trying to distract you.

- People who are jostling you on buses, trains, or subways.

Avoid potentially dangerous situations

To avoid a situation that could lead to a personal attack, stay away from:

- Shrubs, trees, and concealed doorways or other areas where people may hide.

- Isolated streets, parking lots, elevators, rest rooms, and Laundromats, especially at night.

- Badly lit or isolated ATM machines at night.

You may want to consider carrying a personal safety aid such as a personal attack alarm, mace, or pepper spray.

Don't be a car-jacking victim

Here are some tips so you won't become a car-jacking victim:

- Look all around you before entering your car in a parking lot or garage.

- Have your car key in hand before entering the lot or garage.

- Look in your back seat before getting in.

- Lock your car doors immediately.

- Leave space between you and the car ahead at traffic lights. This will give you room to get away should someone approach you.

- If someone does approach your car, be prepared to blare your horn, flash your lights, and step on the gas.

Don't leave anything of value in your car.

Protect Your Home While You're Away

- Buy and use an alarm system, preferably with an external remote. This kind of alarm is a small price to pay for peace of mind and the security of your family and your belongings.

- Check the locks on your doors and windows; replace any that aren't working properly.

- Equip all your windows, especially double-hung windows, with locks or braces.

- Equip the track of sliding doors with a pin stop.

- Use outside lighting around your house to light hidden areas.

- Set your home alarm before leaving and hook it to an automatic dialer if you don't have security monitoring.

- Stop your paper and mail delivery when you're traveling.

- Ask a neighbor to remove anything thrown in your yard or in front of your door in your absence.

- Attach a timer to a few lights in different parts of your house.

- Don't close all your curtains. This usually indicates that no one is home.

Part VII

Traveling Abroad

Travel Documents You Must Have

Travel document requirements vary from country to country, but when you leave the U.S., you will need the following: a passport or other proof of citizenship, plus a visa or a tourist card. (When you enter a foreign country, you may also need evidence that you have enough money for your stay there and/or have an ongoing or return ticket.)

You need a valid passport

A U.S. citizen needs a passport to depart or enter the United States and to enter and depart from most foreign countries. (Your travel agent or airline can tell you if you need a passport for the country you plan to visit.) Even if you are not required to have a passport to visit a country, U.S. Immigration requires you to prove your U.S. citizenship and identity when you reenter the United States.

These documents verify proof of U.S. citizenship:

- A U.S. passport
- An expired U.S. passport
- A certified copy of your birth certificate
- A Certificate of Naturalization
- A Certificate of Citizenship
- A Report of Birth Abroad of a Citizen of the United States.

A valid driver's license or a government identification card that includes a photo or a physical description is adequate to prove your identity, but it is *not* proof of citizenship.

If your passport will expire within six months of your travel dates, you may not be permitted to enter certain countries. (If you return to the United States with an expired passport, you will be subject to a passport waiver fee.)

Getting a Passport

You can get a passport at one of the 13 U.S. government passport agencies, or from one of the 2,500+ state and federal courts, of from the 900+ U.S. post offices.

Apply for your passport several months before your trip and allow at least two additional weeks for each visa that you have requested. (It's a good idea to obtain your visas before you leave the United States because you may not be able to obtain visas for certain countries once you have departed.)

Here are some things you should know about applying for a passport:

- If you are a first-time passport applicant and are age 13 or older, you must apply in person. (Under age 13, a parent or legal guardian may appear on your behalf.)

- You can apply by mail if you were issued a passport within the past 12 years and if you were older than 18 years at the time it was issued. To apply by mail, use application form DSP-82.

What you need to bring

To apply for a passport you need to bring:

- A completed, but unsigned, passport application (form DSP-11).

- Proof of U.S. citizenship. You can use either a previous passport or a certified copy of your birth certificate. (If you were born abroad, a Certificate of Naturalization, a Certificate of Citizenship, Report of Birth Abroad of a U.S. Citizen, or a Certificate of Birth (Form FS-545 or DS-1350) will confirm proof of citizenship.)

Proof of identity

You must also establish your identity to the satisfaction of the person accepting your passport application. The following items are generally acceptable documents of identity if they contain your signature and if they readily identify you by physical description or photograph:

- A previous U.S. passport
- A Certificate of Naturalization or a Certificate of Citizenship
- A valid driver's license
- A government (federal, state, municipal) — identification card.

You need photographs

Present two, identical, 2" x 2", black and white or color photographs of yourself taken within the past 6 months. They must show a front view against a plain, light background.

The cost of a passport

The fee for a 10-year passport for a first-time applicant who is over the age of 18 is $65. (The $10 execution fee is included.) For persons under the age of 18, a five-year passport costs $40. You can pay with cash, personal check, bank draft, or money order.

Apply by mail

You may also apply by mail if:

- You have been issued a passport within 12 years prior to your new application.
- You are able to submit your most recent U.S. passport with your new application.
- Your previous passport was issued on or after your 18th birthday.
- You use the same name as that on your most recent passport or you have had your name changed by marriage or court order.

To apply for a passport by mail, you'll need to obtain an Application for Passport by Mail form (Form DSP-82) from one of the offices accepting applications or from your travel agent and complete the information requested. The cost is $55. (The $10 acceptance fee is not required for applicants eligible to apply by mail.)

When you receive your passport, sign it right away!

To get more information about passports, you can order a brochure entitled "Passports: Applying for Them the Easy Way" from the Federal Consumer Information Center in Pueblo, CO 81009. The cost is 50 cents each.

Obtaining Visas

A visa is an endorsement or stamp placed in your passport by a foreign government that permits you to visit that country for a specified purpose and a limited length of time. To obtain a visa, apply directly to the embassy or nearest consulate of each country you plan to visit, or consult a travel agent.

Health Insurance When Traveling Abroad

If you become seriously ill or are injured while you're traveling overseas, obtaining medical treatment and hospital care can be very costly. Check with your health insurance carrier before you leave the United States to see what benefits, if any, you will be provided.

If your health insurance policy does not cover you abroad, you can purchase a temporary, short-term health and emergency assistance policy. (One of the benefits that are included in a health and emergency assistance policy is coverage for medical evacuation to the United States.) To find out more about short-term health and emergency assistance policies, contact your travel agent or your health insurance company.

Bring a letter from your doctor

If you have any pre-existing medical conditions and will be traveling abroad, bring along a letter from your doctor that describes your condition. The letter should include information about any prescription medicine that you must take. With any luck, this letter will be sufficient for you to bring the medication into the foreign country.

Leave any medication in its original containers, labels and all.

If you become ill while you're overseas

Should you should become ill or be injured while you're overseas, contact the nearest U.S. embassy or consulate and ask them for a list of local doctors, dentists, medical specialists, clinics and hospitals. If your illness or injury is serious, the consul can help you find medical assistance and can contact your family or friends and notify them of your condition. A consul can also assist in the transfer of funds from the United States.

Dealing with Money

This entry covers the stuff you need to remember when using the various forms of money you'll be carrying abroad.

Traveler's checks

Take most of your money in traveler's checks; it's safer.

Record the serial number, denomination and the date and location of the issuing bank or agency. Keep one copy of this information in a safe and separate place at home and a second copy with you, but don't keep it with your traveler's checks. If you lose your traveler's checks, you can get replacements quickly.

Credit cards

Bring credit cards that can be used for purchases and cash advances worldwide. Bring along a copy of the credit cards' numbers and don't keep the list with the credit cards.

If your credit cards or traveler's checks are lost or stolen, immediately notify to the credit card companies and notify the local police.

Foreign currency

Before you depart, purchase a small amount of foreign currency to use for buses, taxis, phones, or tips when you first arrive in a foreign city. Foreign exchange facilities at airports may be closed when your flight arrives. You can purchase foreign currency at some U.S. banks, at foreign exchange firms, or at foreign exchange windows or even vending machines at many international airports in the United States.

Emergency funds

Should you need emergency funds, bring the telephone number for your U.S. bank with you so that you can have money transferred to you.

Protecting Your Valuables

Carry your belongings in a secure manner. When you're walking down a crowded street, be very careful. If you're carrying a shoulder bag, you should keep it tucked under your arm and held securely by the strap. Instead of putting your wallet in your pants' pocket, wear a money belt.

Protecting your passport

Your passport is the most valuable document you will carry abroad. It confirms your U.S. citizenship. Guard it carefully. When you must carry your passport, hide it securely on your person. Do not leave it in a handbag or an exposed pocket. Whenever possible, leave your passport in the hotel safe, not in an empty hotel room or packed in your luggage. One family member should *not* carry all the passports for the entire family.

Leave an itinerary

Leave a detailed itinerary (with names, addresses, and phone numbers of persons and places to be visited) with relatives, friends, and/or business associates in the United States so that they can reach you in an emergency. Also include a photocopy of your passport information page.

Make a list of all your important numbers: your passport information, your credit card numbers, your traveler's checks, and airline ticket numbers. Leave a copy at home and carry a copy with you — separate from your valuables.

Leave your valuables at home

Don't bring anything on your trip that you would hate to lose. Leave your expensive jewelry, family photographs, or objects of sentimental value at home.

Driver's license and auto insurance

Many countries do not recognize a U.S. driver's license. If you intend to drive overseas, check with the embassy or consulate of the countries you will be visiting to get information about their driver's license, road permit, and auto insurance requirements.

Bring proof of prior possession for foreign-made items

If you're planning to take foreign-made personal articles abroad — such as watches, cameras, or video recorders — bring along proof of ownership (a receipt, bill of sale, an insurance policy, or a jeweler's appraisal). Otherwise, these items could be subject to duty and taxes when you return to the U.S.

Reconfirming Your Plane Reservations

When traveling overseas, reconfirm your return reservation at least 72 hours before departure. If your name does not appear on the reservations list, you may not be able to get on your departure flight. When you confirm your reservations in person, ask for a written confirmation. And if you confirm it by phone, ask for the person's name and position and write down the date and time of the call.

Dealing with Immigration and Customs

When you go through Immigration and Customs, have your passport and other documents — such as an International Certificate of Vaccination, a medical letter, or a Customs certificate of registration for foreign-made personal articles — ready. If you need to support your customs declaration, have your receipts available.

Pack your baggage in a way to make the inspection by the Customs agent easier.

Appendix
Frequently Called Numbers

*1*f you decide to carry this book with you when you travel (as I hope you will), I've provided a place for you to write down phone numbers and other important information. So not only does this book contain a plethora of great tips, it will also contain your personal information, which means that you may only need to carry this one book with you when you travel.

Your Favorite Airlines' Reservations Phone Numbers

Name   *Phone Number*

_____

_____

_____

_____

_____

Your Favorite Airlines' Flight Confirmation Phone Numbers

Name   *Phone Number*

_____

_____

_____

_____

_____

Your Favorite Car Rental Companies

Name	Phone Number

Your Favorite Taxi or Limo Services

Name	City	Phone Number

Your Favorite Hotels

Name	City	Phone Number

Your Favorite Restaurants

Name	City	Phone Number

Your Favorite Out-of-Town Friends

Name	City	Phone Number

Technical Support Numbers for Your Favorite Computer Software

Name	Phone Number

Your Most Important Business and Personal Phone Numbers

Name	Phone Number

Friends and Relatives

Name	Phone Number

Index

•G•

•H•

•Q•

•R•

IDG BOOKS WORLDWIDE REGISTRATION CARD

RETURN THIS REGISTRATION CARD FOR FREE CATALOG

Title of this book: Time Management For Dummies Survival Guide

My overall rating of this book: ❑ Very good [1] ❑ Good [2] ❑ Satisfactory [3] ❑ Fair [4] ❑ Poor [5]

How I first heard about this book:

❑ Found in bookstore; name: [6]   ❑ Book review: [7]

❑ Advertisement: [8]   ❑ Catalog: [9]

❑ Word of mouth; heard about book from friend, co-worker, etc.: [10]   ❑ Other: [11]

What I liked most about this book:

What I would change, add, delete, etc., in future editions of this book:

Other comments:

Number of computer books I purchase in a year: ❑ 1 [12] ❑ 2-5 [13] ❑ 6-10 [14] ❑ More than 10 [15]

I would characterize my computer skills as: ❑ Beginner [16] ❑ Intermediate [17] ❑ Advanced [18] ❑ Professional [19]

I use ❑ DOS [20] ❑ Windows [21] ❑ OS/2 [22] ❑ Unix [23] ❑ Macintosh [24] ❑ Other: [25]_____
(please specify)

I would be interested in new books on the following subjects:
(please check all that apply, and use the spaces provided to identify specific software)

❑ Word processing: [26]   ❑ Spreadsheets: [27]

❑ Data bases: [28]   ❑ Desktop publishing: [29]

❑ File Utilities: [30]   ❑ Money management: [31]

❑ Networking: [32]   ❑ Programming languages: [33]

❑ Other: [34]

I use a PC at (please check all that apply): ❑ home [35] ❑ work [36] ❑ school [37] ❑ other: [38] _____

The disks I prefer to use are ❑ 5.25 [39] ❑ 3.5 [40] ❑ other: [41]_____

I have a CD ROM: ❑ yes [42] ❑ no [43]

I plan to buy or upgrade computer hardware this year: ❑ yes [44] ❑ no [45]

I plan to buy or upgrade computer software this year: ❑ yes [46] ❑ no [47]

Name: Business title: [48]

Type of Business: [49]

Address (❑ home [50] ❑ work [51] /Company name:

Street/Suite#

City [52]/State [53]/Zipcode [54]:   Country [55]

❑ **I liked this book!**
You may quote me by name in future IDG Books Worldwide promotional materials.

My daytime phone number is _____

IDG BOOKS

THE WORLD OF COMPUTER KNOWLEDGE

❏ YES!

Please keep me informed about IDG's World
of Computer Knowledge. Send me the latest
IDG Books catalog.